101010**101**0101010101010101
SOFTWARE
PACKAGES
TO USE IN YOUR LIBRARY

Descriptions, Evaluations, and Practical Advice

By
PATRICK R. DEWEY

AMERICAN LIBRARY ASSOCIATION
Chicago and London 1987

Designed by Charles Bozett

Composed by Pam Frye Typesetting, Inc.,
    in English Times and Eras on an MCS/100
    Compugraphic/8400 typesetting system.

Printed on 50-pound Glatfelter, a
    pH-neutral stock, and bound in
    10-point Carolina cover stock
    Edwards Brothers, Inc.
    ∞

Library of Congress Cataloging-in-Publication Data

Dewey, Patrick R., 1949–
    101 software packages to use in your library.

    Includes index.
    1. Library science—Computer programs—Catalogs.
2. Libraries—Automation—Computer programs—Catalogs.
3. Microcomputers—Library applications—Computer
programs—Catalogs. I. Title. II. Title: One hundred
one software packages to use in your library.
III. Title: One hundred and one software packages to use
in your library.
Z678.9.A3D48   1987   025'.02'0285   86-22310
ISBN 0-8389-0455-6

This book is dedicated to my two dogs,
Hardware and Software.
Though they supported me every inch of the
way, I'm afraid that they don't think much
of computers.

Contents

Acknowledgments

I would like to thank all of the vendors who supplied information and products for their help. In the preparation of the manuscript, I would like to thank the many people at ALA, including Bettina MacAyeal, who persuaded me to write this book in the first place; Herbert Bloom; and Helen Cline and her excellent staff.

Introduction

This book was written for several good reasons: It is the only low-cost library-related software directory in existence; in addition, it is the only directory which tells very much about the software it inventories, and from firsthand. Every effort was made to see the actual software — to examine it myself — rather than rely on third-party reviews. All of the software in this directory is recommended, even though limitations and problems are pointed out. In this volume, more than bibliographic data are given, for each entry includes as much of the following information as possible:

Title	Capacity, when appropriate
Vendor	Description
Price	Nature and quality of documentation
Hardware requirements	Similar or related programs
Uses in library	Additional sources of information
Grade level, when appropriate	

Some of these data were difficult to document. For instance, it was originally intended to describe a library where each package is in use, but this turned out to be so difficult that the intention was abandoned in all but a few cases. "Capacity" was easy to find, except when it was not noted in the program documentation. A phone call to the vendor would sometimes provide the information, but sometimes even the vendor did not know.

This book, in describing a wide range of software for library use, provides a "feel" for how the software works and how it fits into the library setting. Some of the software is library-specific, some is not. My interest was not in software that had been specifically created for library use, but software which could solve a problem or do a job in a library. Obviously, many standard, nonlibrary software packages fall within this scope, and so word processors, database managers, and spreadsheets are found alongside catalog card programs, acquisitions systems, circulation systems, programs which test new employees on the library classification system, specialized library inventory systems, and much more. A few programs for use with patrons are included, but all are related to library activity in some way (e.g., library instruction programs). As necessary, I have cited related programs (in some categories).

The software was chosen in several ways. First, a wide variety of sources was used to find software which libraries actually use. I read a great many microcomputer periodicals for libraries and library journals which contain reviews or discussions of software. I also searched many other sources of microcomputer software information including mainstream (nonlibrary) microcomputer journals, magazines, and software directories. In this way, I discovered titles such as *The Newsroom, The Print Shop, Puzzles and Posters,* etc. Some of the software is reviewed with an eye toward what libraries *can* do with certain packages, rather than what they *are* doing.

At the beginning of each chapter are comments and guidelines for selection of the type of software described in that chapter. A great variety of software has been included, at various prices, since an elementary school library might not be able to use the same cataloging program as a public library, nor be able to spend as much money on its purchase. When appropriate, the descriptions indicate for which type of library a program is recommended, though this is usually self-evident.

Two basic machines, the Apple II series and the IBM PC, were the principal microcomputers in the search process, but many software packages have other versions and applications as well, and these are noted.

Software data are accessible by title, microcomputer, vendor, and application.

Sources of Additional Information

An excellent bibliography of microcomputer use in libraries is *Library Applications of Microcomputers: A Bibliography,* prepared for the Missouri Library Association (MLA Administrative Office, Parkade Plaza, Suite 9, Columbia, MO 65201) by Lorna Mitchel et al. (November 1984). Other sources are:

Nolan, Jeanne E. *Micro Software Report, Library Edition.* Vol. 3, 1984–85. Meckler Publishing, 11 Ferry Lane West, Westport, CT 06880. $97.50.
Microcomputers for Libraries: Product Review and Procurement Guide. James E. Rush Associates, Inc., 2223 Carnage Rd., Powell, OH 43506. $83. Includes updates. Separate volumes are on serials control, circulation control, public service, acquisitions, management services, interlibrary loan, cataloging, and system integration. $59.50 each.
Chen, Ching-chih. *MicroUse Directory: Software.* MicroUse Information, 1400 Commonwealth Ave., West Newton, MA 02165. $99.50

Mason, Bob. *The Micro Consumer: Library Software: A Software Selection.* November 1984. Metrics Research Corporation, 11000 Cedar Ave., Cleveland, OH 44106. $25.

Guidelines for Selecting Software

Keeping up with new software is like trying to hit a moving target: the field is always changing and updates are constant. When software is purchased for in-house library use, a number of common elements should be kept in mind at all times, and some of these are listed below. However, it is rare that all of these criteria can be satisfied for any single piece of software. When more than one package is available from different vendors, these general categories or considerations will assist in the selection process:

Documentation. Is it clear? Does it cover all the important points? Some programs are "self-documenting"; that is, they contain all the important instructions online.

User friendly. Is the program easy to learn and operate, or confusing and cumbersome?

Capacity. Will the program hold and process as many records as needed? Will it support a fixed disk for mass storage, if required?

Speed. If sorting is a program function and the program must process many data (say 800 records), how long does it take? Clearly, the faster the sort time, the more quickly the library's work will be accomplished. Besides sort time, factors which enter into the speed of a program include the number and type of menus, cursor movement, keystrokes, scrolling, etc.

Vendor support. Many software programs must be purchased through the mail, so finding a local vendor who can help out may be difficult. Major programs, such as *WordStar* or *dBase*, should be purchased from a local vendor who can install the program and provide backup support. The best of all possible worlds is to purchase the whole thing, software and hardware, from the same local vendor. Unfortunately, few local vendors sell everything, and almost none sells library-specific software. One alternative is a demonstration package, when available, or a 30- or 60-day return privilege, which some vendors offer. "Demos" are usually free or inexpensive, or their cost may sometimes be applied toward the purchase price of the complete package.

Hardware compatibility. If hardcopy is required, make sure that the program is compatible with your printer. Other types of compatibility include the make and model of the microcomputer, number and size of the disk drives, RAM memory, 80-column card, modem, and monitor.

Sophistication. Does the package have all the required features? A simple checklist will solve many problems in advance. Attempt to come as close to the ideal as possible. Analyze several packages before you make any selection.

Integration. If certain features, such as mailmerge, graphics, database capabilities, etc., are required, make sure that the program has these features or can integrate with modules that do.

References. Before purchasing an expensive program, such as a total circulation control system, get a reference from another librarian. Library user groups or statewide directories are good sources for references. A list of many library user groups has been appended to this book.

Sometimes it is difficult to find a library program which will do exactly what is required. This type of problem is solved (when it can be solved at all) by resorting to nonlibrary software directories. Just because a program was not written with libraries in mind does not mean that it won't do the job.

Sources of General Information

Glossbrenner, Alfred. *How to Buy Software.* St. Martin's Press, 1984.
Glossbrenner, Alfred. *How to Get Free Software.* St. Martin's Press, 1984.

Guidelines for Selecting Hardware

In a nutshell, for purposes of selection, a computer consists of a central processing unit (CPU), monitor, random access memory (RAM), read only memory (ROM), mass storage devices, a printer, and a modem. Many other devices may be added later, but it is generally wise to purchase as much of the system as possible in the beginning and at the same place. If something does not function, the vendor will not be able to blame someone else's component. Also, a better deal can usually be struck when everything is bought at once (much like buying your car in one piece, as opposed to buying it in a parts shop). Nearly always, some software is included, and, depending upon the machine, *WordStar* or another word processor may be "thrown in" for free, as well as graphics packages, or even an integrated software system. This kind of acquisition is known as "bundled" (as opposed to "bungled").

Hardware is that part of a computer which you see, the exterior or physical parts. *Software* is the set of instructions which tell the computer what to do. The part of the software that controls the whole operation is the *operating system,* usually referred to as the DOS (for disk operating system). It controls the whole show, from control of the printer and the disk drives to the storage and retrieval of files. (It is different from a *computer language,* such as BASIC or Pascal, in which a computer program is written.)

A computer may be run with only one operating system (though most have two or more), but many programs. CP/M is one popular operating system, MS-DOS is another. The new standard operating system for the Apple II series is ProDOS.

To run a program that is written for a particular operating system, it is necessary to have that system in the computer (unless you are using a special program, such as *Extra K,* it is possible to have only one operating system in a computer at any time). Since some systems are made to run with only a certain central processing unit (a CPU is the "brain" of the microcomputer and handles logical decisions, arithmetic, input/output, and timing), the proper CPU must be in the microcomputer. However, it is possible to purchase what are known as "co-processors," or a CPU on a special circuit board. The board simply plugs into the main board of the microcomputer.

As noted, other hardware parts of the microcomputer include the random access memory, or RAM. RAM is the amount of internal storage space available to the microcomputer for program or data storage. It resides *inside* the microcomputer. RAM, which is alterable from the keyboard, changes as required. However, another type of internal storage is read only memory (ROM), which does *not* change. It is permanently stored or embedded in the chips of the microcomputer. ROM generally consists of utility programs or computer languages—programs that are used on a regular basis as part of the basic computer system.

External or mass storage consists of disk drives, either hard (fixed) or floppy. Both types come in various sizes and may hold from about 100K (a K, or kilobyte, is 1000 bytes; a byte is 1 character) to many megabytes (or millions of bytes). (Incidentally, a gigabyte is 1 billion bytes.)

Some computers come with a hard disk drive that is built in—usually 5 megabytes, but sometimes 10 or 20. Most library applications require two 5-inch drives (or one 5-inch and one fixed or hard drive), though many one-drive applications may be purchased. It is always desirable to own a second disk drive. The size of the drive does not determine capability, since a 3-inch disk may hold more data than a 5- or an 8-inch disk, and a 5-inch disk may hold more data than an 8-inch disk. It depends upon the drive. The cost of fixed disks has plummeted, so that some of them are not much more expensive than 5-inch drives.

The monitor displays the output (softcopy) to the user. While a few microcomputers still use a 40-column display, most now display 80 columns across the screen, giving output more nearly the look of a real page if an appropriate 80-column card (circuit board or addition) is installed. Some programs display up to 70 columns, with or without a screen that has an 80-column capability and with or without an 80-column card. This is done with "softvideo," the use of high-resolution graphics in place of a true character set. General library work is best served with an 80-column display.

Making all of these decisions requires an understanding of the microcomputers currently on the market, as well as a comprehensive look at the applications software and the requirements of the library where the system will be installed. It will be necessary to gather pertinent data, make comparisons, ask questions, and read microcomputer books and journals. A decision may be made hurriedly, especially if someone on the staff is acquainted with microcomputers, but the more time spent on selection, the better the chance of selecting the right machine and the right applications programs. Suffice it to say that it is more complicated than buying an automobile, sometimes more expensive, and therefore ought to take much longer.

Here are a few rules of thumb:

1. It is better to purchase a machine that is expandable than one which is not.
2. The more RAM, the better.
3. Backup or vendor support is essential.
4. It is a good idea to purchase a microcomputer that has a large market share.
5. When a modem is bought, 300/1200 baud is better than 300 baud.
6. When you purchase a printer, decide in advance if letter quality is necessary (see below).

All about Printers

The weakest link in the hardware/software chain is often the printer. Poor-quality print will destroy the best work of any applications package. Below are some hints to aid in selection of a good printer.

First, there are two types of printers: dot matrix and daisywheel (there are a few other types as well, but consult other books and magazines for more in-depth coverage of this subject). The dot matrix has traditionally been the printer of poorer quality, the letters being made up of dots and not fully formed. In fact, some early models had "pseudo descenders," or letters that did not go below the print line (e.g., "y"s, "g"s, "p"s), cleverly formed characters that fooled us into believing they were the real thing. Daisywheel print quality is about the same as that of a good electric typewriter; a small hammer hits a character on a wheel, which in turn strikes the ribbon. The difference between the dot and the daisywheel—namely, the quality of print—has blurred in recent years. Dot matrix printers now approach letter quality, and are even sold with the label "Near Letter Quality." Newer printers employ an inkjet process and lasers. One advantage of the latter group is that their print quality is comparable to type.

Because it is important to analyze just what capabilities are needed in the printer, here's a short checklist of the most important. It is usually possible to get most of them in a single printer at a reasonable price.

True proportional spacing	Carriage width adjustment
Subscript/superscript	Alarm signal for "out of paper"
Tractor feed	Alarm signal for "paper off track"
Friction feed	Selection of print wheels
Speed	Graphics (dot matrix only)
Bidirectional printing	Print buffer (at least 2K)
(can speed things up)	Character-per-inch adjustment
Boldface printing	Cut sheet feeder

Some of these features may have to be purchased as extras; and it is a good idea to make sure that they are available, even if they are not purchased immediately. Some items are mutually exclusive: a daisywheel cannot generate graphics; a dot matrix printer does not need print wheels (though it can usually produce many styles of type or fonts, either by program control or dip switches, which are special controls).

In addition, be sure that a convenient source of service (and ribbons) exists. It should not be necessary to mail the printer (or microcomputer) away for service. To do so would mean considerable downtime.

Certain types of work may benefit from the purchase of special circuit boards or printer cards which create very large print buffers. With such cards (also known as "spoolers," for "simultaneous peripheral operation online"), entire manuscripts may be "dumped" into the buffer for printing while the computer is freed for other work.

All printers are noisy, and especially a daisywheel; so check into buying an acoustic or noise-reduction cabinet. It may save the eardrums of everyone in the library.

Sources of Additional Information

Darnall, W. H., and D. B. Corner. *The Epson Connection: Apple.* Reston, 1984 (11480 Sunset Hills Rd., Reston, VA 22090).

Nath, Sanjiva K., et al. *Buyer's Guide to Printers.* Tab, 1985 (Blue Ridge Summit, PA 17214).

"What to Look For in a Printer," *Personal Computing,* August 1984, p. 153.

Good Work Habits for Good Computing

Good work habits are like gold. Bad work habits contain the seeds of their own destruction.

Backups. One of the most important things is to protect the work that is "saved to disk" by making *backup* copies. This may sometimes seem bothersome, or even a waste of time, but if it is not learned now, it will be learned in the long run through painful experience.

Avoiding disk woes. Floppy diskettes are fragile, and should be handled very carefully. A magnetic medium, diskettes react to a static or magnetic charge. Just walking across a carpet can build a destructive static charge. One solution is always to touch the case of the computer before beginning work, to discharge any static buildup. Do not carry diskettes in your hand across a carpet. (An antistatic spray is available, but it is necessary to spray every day.) Transport diskettes only in a plastic container.

Backup copies should not be stored with the primary set, since adverse conditions could obliterate both sets.

Organizing files. The most important process associated with organizing files is retrieval. For most libraries, this will be no great problem, since most working files, or templates, will reside on one or just a few disks. For large operations, however, it might be necessary to use many disks or a large fixed disk of 10 or 20 megabytes. In such cases, the simplest thing is to put similar types of work on the same disk and label each disk accordingly: recent correspondence, board minutes, proposals for an LSCA grant, etc.

A fixed disk may usually be "partitioned" into several logical drives. In such an arrangement, the user will have the equivalent of many smaller drives. Some operating systems, such as ProDOS and MS-DOS, allow for "tree" or "hierarchical" directories. This type of system makes more efficient use of hard disk drives, with more flexibility in the preparation of files and the storage of data.

To the user, it still appears as though the drive is divided into smaller volumes, but they "stretch" according to the space needed (each volume expands to accommodate whatever space is required). Such systems possess "automatic partitioning" instead of the "fixed volume arrangement" of apple DOS 3.3. (These procedures are described in the manuals for the operating systems.)

Disk care. The 5-inch disk drive is the most common, but most considerations apply to 8-inch drives as well. (Hard disk drives are another matter altogether and are discussed separately below.) Except for a few special programs, a disk is only infrequently in use (when the disk drive is writing or reading a program or data), which accounts for its long life. Normally, a disk gets very little use during one sitting at the keyboard. Its typical life is many years, though some disks are defective right out of the box, or "blow" after a very few uses. (There's no explaining this, but it *does* explain the need for backup copies of everything.)

When the data on a disk are "stale" and no longer useful, the disk should not be thrown away, but saved and treated as a new disk—reformatted and used again, unless deep grooves are evident on the surface (where the drive head has rubbed). Then it is time to consider disposing of the disk. (Old diskettes make great mobiles when they are tied with string and decorated in different colors.)

Diskettes should be stored in a container which will not squeeze them together, but allow them to be conveniently removed or replaced and labeled. They should be free from dust and kept away from heat, cold, kids, dogs, cats, smoke, and food, and never scratched, pressed, or laid flat for long periods, since disks stored in this fashion tend to warp.

Basic Computer Care

Thus we come to the computer itself. What can be done to protect it? If the machine did not come with a fan, one should be installed. For the Apple, a fan is relatively inexpensive ($30 to $60) and will probably double the life of electronic components.

Carelessness during the installation of circuit boards and other devices is the greatest cause of problems with circuitry. Exercise extreme caution, since even pros "mess up" and burn out circuit boards.

Aside from diskettes, the part likeliest to fail is the disk drive, a mechanical component. Sometimes the failure is as simple as a dirty read/write head; sometimes it's more complicated: bad chips or a shortened circuit board. Disk drives have had pencils, paper, and all sorts of things (including diskettes) jammed into them by the public when no one was looking. If the machine is not in a public area, this last group of problems may never arise. However, people wander into unauthorized areas, so it is a good idea to keep machines bolted down and covered when they are not in use (children have managed to stick toy blocks into our acquisitions microcomputer when no one was looking). Bad chips and other electronic problems must be diagnosed and corrected by a professional—which is why it is so important to have a local vendor who can perform such a service.

Hard disk drives bring special problems. If, for instance, the disk head "crashes," all of the data may be lost. If, for any reason, the disk is not accessible, *all* data are lost until accessibility is restored. To avoid this problem, it is necessary to backup a hard disk by using many, many floppies, or a videotape system. Cartridge or removable hard disk systems can provide their own backup system, but, in such a case, even the backup is not accessible until the disk drive is restored to working condition.

Vendor service is very important—the closer the vendor the better. Ideally—as has been stated—if all hardware is purchased from the same vendor, it is easier to have everything repaired at the same place.

Ergonomics is simply the comfort, efficiency, and safety of the computer workspace. Employees can suffer considerable fatigue if their chairs and other equipment are not adjustable to their needs. Chairs are now available which tilt, lean, and adjust to any height or level.

The bad effects of *monitors* and *glare* have been controversial for some time now. Aside from any radiation that may be given off by the monitor, glare— and eyestrain—can result from improper lighting or excessive reflection. Putting the workstation in an area which has properly controlled lighting can eliminate most such problems.

Security of hardware is of great concern. It should be possible to lock the equipment up at the end of the day, at least in an office. All microcomputer equipment should be bolted to a table or desk, and there are many special devices for this purpose.

Food, drink, or smoke—needless to say—should *not* be allowed in the computer area.

Sources of Additional Information

Atwater, Dorothea. *First Aid for Your IBM PC.* Ballantine, 1985.

Beechhold, Henry F. *The Plain English Repair and Maintenance Guide for Home Computers.* Simon & Schuster, 1984.

Health Hazards of CRTs, 2nd ed. Ryan Research International, 1983 (1593 Filbert Ave., Chico, CA 95926).

Makower, Joel, and Edward Murry. *Everybody's Computer Fix-it Book.* Quantum/Doubleday, 1985.

Schleifer, Lawrence M., and Steven L. Sauter. "Controlling Glare Problems in the VDT Work Environment," *Library Hi Tech,* issue 12, 1985, p. 21.

Wagenvoord, James. *ComputerSpace.* Perigee Books, 1984.

Zaks, Rodney. *Don't! (or, How to Care for Your Computer).* Sybex, 1981 (2344 Sixth St., Berkeley, CA 94710).

Acquisitions

Introduction

Acquisitions software, in the end, is database management software; it maintains records (of one sort or another) to help a library automate, in part or in whole, the acquisition of materials. Like everything else, this may be accomplished in more than one way. Just how a particular library should go about it depends largely upon the type of library, the available resources (both skill and hardware), and what it wishes to accomplish.

Some libraries have only the simplest acquisitions needs, such as maintenance of an order file with basic order data (price, order date, call number, etc.). Larger libraries usually need to "track" ordered materials, beginning with the time at which the request was put into the ordering system until the material is (or is not) received by the library – through the generation of regular reports of encumbered and expended funds, ordered price versus actual price, to which department the material should go after it has been received, etc. These capabilities go far beyond the generation of a simple order list.

The two basic forms of acquisition are do-it-yourself and off-the-shelf programs. Neither way is necessarily easier, nor does either way imply lack of sophistication. Both categories contain programs which are flexible to some degree. Certainly, either category may also be expensive, costing as much as $1000 or more.

Do-It-Yourself

Let's start with do-it-yourself. These programs are not specifically geared to library needs, but were created for a much wider business or personal computer market. They include *dBase, List Handler, Appleworks, PFS:File*, etc. The program that is easiest to use is *List Handler*, which libraries have used to produce a standing order file (see reference below). It will also produce customized form letters and labels. A program such as this, or any similar easy-to-use database system, may be best for the small library that is interested only in maintaining a list of basic information.

A more formidable program is *dBase*. On one level, *dBase* is easy to use. Anyone can install the system, "create" a data base "structure," and begin to "input data" in just a few minutes. The list that is created may be "indexed" and "reports" generated. The report format is trickier, but it will eventually become clear. The program is *not* user friendly. Its popularity lies not in its excellent list handling capability, but in its programming language. By producing "command files," which look and act like ordinary computer programs (e.g., BASIC or Pascal), it is possible to get *dBase* to produce a program of immense power and sophistication. However, it is this very programming structure (also known as "structured programming") that causes many problems. In particular, it will be necessary to spend long hours programming and debugging. This program is not for the casual database user or the computer neophyte.

dBase is so widely used, however, that many *dBase* "programs" (templates) are available from many sources. Ashton-Tate, the manufacturer of *dBase*, publishes a catalog of such programs ("Application Junction"). Many online systems, such The Source or CompuServe, also provide this type of user group interaction, and such programs may be downloaded free (for the price of your online connect charges and local phone call). They may usually be changed to fit a particular need or circumstance—assuming that one knows how to make such changes.

Off-the-Shelf

Off-the-shelf programs—those which are available for a specific purpose, with no programming required—include *Accession Plus, Orderit, Bib-Base/Acq,* and many others. *Accession Plus* merely automates the production of a bibliography; *Orderit,* though intended for small libraries, has great power for such a modest package. It permits easy input of titles and listing, or search by publisher, title, and author.

Bib-Base/Acq is a spectacular and full-fledged system for tracking acquisitions from start to finish, producing reports at any point, and providing statistical data. It also uses MARC-tagged fields, for libraries which have this advanced need. In addition, it is "integrated," or, more simply, part of a family of software (by the same company) that work together, forming a sophisticated overall software environment. This program is expensive (at least when compared with those above), but it is user friendly and menu driven. It works only with an IBM PC (or a compatible).

Notes on Selecting Acquisitions Software

Of primary importance in selecting software for acquisitions or cataloging is determining the library's needs, then matching those needs with available systems. A needs list can most often be compiled after discussion of the current system with the acquisitions or cataloging staff. (The staff should be involved in every selection process, and not just in the beginning.) As systems are considered, they should be analyzed by staff to make sure that they meet standards and contain all desired features. Brainstorming sessions are a good way to begin, but simple narratives of the present work process by those engaged in it, are a sound basis for beginning. Beyond this, it is necessary to *examine* the various software packages in order to make every effort to improve upon the current system, not just automate it.

Software by Size of Library

Small libraries (Right On modules):
  Accession Plus
  Catalogit
  Orderit
Medium-sized libraries:
  Ettacq
  dBase (or other database manager)
  List Handler
  VisiCalc (templates)
Large libraries:
  Bib-Base/Acq
  dBase (or other database manager)
  Ettacq

Acquisitions Routine

Ordering list of books, periodicals, and continuations
Checking for duplicates
Generating order slips or letters
Fund accounting
Coding (e.g., type of media)
Claiming unreceived materials
Accumulating orders for bulk ordering (e.g., in the case of expected grant)
Producing statistical ordering data (who orders how many books, etc.)
Maintaining encumbered/expended file

Checking books in on arrival
Integrating other programs (e.g., catalog card production, MARC-tagged fields)
Boolean searching

Sources of Additional Information

Bjorner, Susan N. "Catalog Card Production: A Comparison of Two Software Packages," *Small Computers in Libraries,* July 1982, p. 1.

Caine, W. "Producing Information Cards for the Card Catalog Using *Apple Writer II," Apple Library Users Group Newsletter,* January 1985, p. 37.

"Catalog Card Printing Program," *Small Computers in Libraries,* November 1982, p. 7.

Frechette, James. "Library Acquisitions on a Micro Scale," *Library Journal,* November 1985, p. 154.

"Small Computer On-Line Acquisitions System (SCOLAS)," *Small Computers in Libraries,* February 1983, p. 2.

Tench, R. Terry. "Catalog Card Production Using *Apple Writer," Apple Library Users Group,* April 1985, p. 55.

Walker, Stephen. "A Microcomputer Based Library Acquisition System," *Small Computers in Libraries,* August 1982, p. 6.

Reviews

Accession Plus

Bib-Base/Acq

Ettacq

MATSS

Orderit

Name:	**Accession Plus**
Program type:	Accession
Vendor:	Right On Programs
Cost:	$40
Hardware requirements:	Apple II series; Commodore 64; IBM PC, XT, PCjr.
Capacity:	Unknown

Description: *Accession Plus* is a straightforward, easy-to-use program for recording new books or printing out subject or author listings for teachers or student lists. Book order information may be recalled by subject, title, author, or call number. A description field is also provided. Publisher and cost are not included as fields. Materials may be entered into the system or deleted. There is no true correction feature, since a record must be deleted from the list and then reentered. Fortunately, this is not a significant drawback for someone who wants an extremely easy-to-use program.

Documentation: Two pages

Name: **Bib-Base/Acq**

Program Type: Acquisitions/bibliographic production

Vendor: Small Library Computing, Inc.

Cost: $895. $45 demonstration package (includes manual) may be applied toward full package purchase later.

Hardware requirements: IBM PC, XT, or AT with 256K, one disk drive, one hard disk, PC-DOS 2.0 or higher. Will run on Radio Shack/Tandy 1000, 1200, Zenith Z150 and Z160, Columbia, Compaq, and other compatibles. Zenith Z110/Z120 version is available.

Capacity: Limited by disk storage capacity (database up to 2 billion characters). Two hundred suppliers may be entered; 200 different funds may be defined; 54 record status codes may be defined; 200 other special codes or "types" may be used for further tracking of expenditures and ordering. Limits are 1000 records on 360K disk drives and 3500 records on 1.2 megabyte (high-density AT) drives. This will vary according to size of records entered (i.e., more short than long records will fit on a disk).

Description: This acquisitions module of a bibliographic database is totally menu driven and, for such a sophisticated system, very easy to operate. Its bibliographic functions provide for variable length data fields and records. Records are indexed by author, title, ISBN, call number, order number, and accession number. There are two types of fields: fixed (predefined) and bibliographic. Fixed fields include dates, price, format, etc. Bibliographic fields are entered by using full-screen text editor (included) with wraparound.

System also maintains tabs on encumbered and expended funds, as well as printing order slips and purchase orders. Items may be tracked from point at which they are ordered to final cataloging process. Lists of unfilled, filled, or other types of orders may be printed on demand. Budgeted amounts may be assigned to each fund, type, and supplier. System keeps track of totals after expenditures and encumbered amounts have been entered.

The select, sort, and list functions allow for reports of almost any type, in numerical order by accession number, by call number (if material has been cataloged), by materials not yet received, by date, etc. *Bib-Base/Marc* (an optional module) will load and use full MARC-format records and output MARC-format records for transfer to other systems. Reports may be printed on 3 × 5 cards (these are not catalog cards) or in a variety of other ways by telling the program how the page should be formatted: offset printed form, determine page headings, and set number of lines per page.

This excellent system is highly sophisticated and flexible, but may represent "overkill" for many small and medium-size libraries. System also takes time to learn to operate, especially if MARC-tagged fields are employed. In any case, big price tag makes it prohibitive for small and budget-conscious institutions.

Documentation: More than 150 pages describe the system in detail, with step-by-step instructions and explanations. Appendix A tells how to handle error messages (start-up errors, operating errors, and indexing errors). Appendix B tells how to create multiple databases (e.g., it is possible to create separate database of titles received in previous years). Appendix D describes order output formats and gives examples of 3 × 5 cards. Several types of forms may be automatically generated, including Order Form, Backup Copy Format, Actual Order Form Format, Order Summary Form, Purchase Order Output Option, or formats may be sent to disk instead of paper. Appendix Z is summary of all MARC tags acceptable to *Bib-Base.*

Related
programs: Other modules in this system—*Bib-Base/Cat, Bib-Base/Text, Bib-Base/Marc, TermMarc, Ultracard*—may be purchased in various combinations.

Name: **Ettacq**

Program type: Acquisitions

Vendor: ETT Library Automations, Inc.

Cost: $1000 (Pricing structure may be significantly lowered soon; check with vendor.)

Hardware
requirements: Apple II series, with 5 megabyte profile hard disk, Apple Imagewriter. Available soon for Macintosh and IBM PC.

Used at: Skokie Public Library
5215 Oakton St.
Skokie, IL 60077
312-673-7774

Capacity: 15,000 records (5,000 each of books, continuations, and periodicals)

Description: This completely menu-driven package is exceptionally easy to use. Only currently available version, however, is for Apple II, which does not provide fund accounting or many sophisticated advantages of *Bib-Base/Acq;* but this package is much easier to learn—a distinct advantage for many small libraries. Some of the features include order-slip generating on continuous feed paper, checking for duplicate orders by author and title, and printing of claim and cancellation notices for overdue orders. Orders may be typed in a batch, corrected, then printed out on special continuous order forms. Reports include On Order, On Claim, In Process, monthly reports of standing orders, serial and periodical orders to be placed, and more.

Vendor file will support 30 vendors, with amount of money encumbered with each, amount spent, number of titles and volumes ordered/received, average number of days to fill order, and average discount percentage. Changes in credit/debit of vendor records are easy to make, and vendor information may be recalled or printed out at any time – and is updated with each new entry. Selector file will hold 30 selectors, with amount of money encumbered/spent, number of titles/volumes selected, and the same credit/debit ability for any field (or view or print selector information). All three files are updated with each entry.

Orders may be placed with following fields: title, author, ISBN, publisher, call number, vendor, four funds and four selectors per order, date ordered, reference number (defined by user), and notes. Orders may also be downloaded from outside optical disk source or maintained in consideration file. Users may enter up to 200 orders at one sitting, with up to 7000 active orders on the disk at one time.

IBM and Macintosh versions (which may be available by time this book is in print) should make it easy to find, print, or edit credit/debit information, updated automatically with each entry.

Documentation: Excellent tutorial/user manual is easy-to-follow, walk-through, looseleaf notebook.

Name: **MATSS** (Midwest Automated Technical Services Software), version 2.0

Program type: Acquisitions

Vendor: Midwest Technical Services

Cost: $3995 for full system. Acquisitions system includes all related Technical Services modules (below), as well as 12 hours of on-site training, manuals, order production, vendor reporting, open order database access, fund accounting, automatic claiming, and cancellation. $50 for demonstration disk and manual (may be applied toward purchase)
Individual modules (Technical Services):
  $300, bibliographic utility and communications interface
  $300, catalog card production
  $800, fund accounting

$150, label production (spine and pocket)
$300, manual data entry
$300, order production
Training and setup:
$800, two days
$250, each additional day

Hardware
requirements: IBM PC, 256K, two disk drives or one disk drive plus hard disk, PC or MS DOS 2.00 or greater, and printer. Will work with IBM compatibles and M300.

Capacity: 32,500 vendors
32,500 accounts
32,500 records in open order file

Description: Version 1.1, a complete acquisitions system, performs fund accounting, catalog card data entry and production, spine and label production, order form production, and serves as communications program for downloading MARC records from online utilities for use with any of program's other functions. Original records (manual entry) may be produced with order/catalog entry program, which includes sophisticated text editor.

The accounting program (available separately) takes its data directly, as orders are placed, and keeps encumbered accounts up to date. Funds may later be unencumbered at the original price and expended at actual price.

Perhaps the most striking aspect is program's ease of use. After a short period of creating a directory and copying the files to your hard disk or floppies, the main menu offers quick and unconfusing movement to any program activity. Other features are password protection and extensive customization. Version 2.0 (not available for preview at this writing) goes beyond the older version in many ways. *MATSS* now supports Library of Congress (2 formats), Dewey, and National Library of Medicine call numbers, bill-to/ship-to addresses, reports displayed to screen or printed out, duplicate order checking, and monochrome or color monitors.

Vendor information: Searchable by name, number, or grouped by fiscal year. Includes quantities and dollar amounts of items on order, filled, and canceled; prints mailing labels; generates purchase orders by author/title or title/author sequence; supports Standard Access Number (SAN); and is capable of electronic transmission of orders to any vendor that accepts BISAC variable record format. Fund accounting supports multiple fiscal years; has three levels for report subtotaling. Summary records keep track of each fund, and special report indicates accounts above or below chosen percentage in expense encumbered or available balance.

Order entry: Purchase orders are numbered automatically; vendor, purchase order number, copies, fund accounts, and comments may be defaulted. Full-screen editor. Reorders may be produced from open order file without rekeying; multiple batches of orders may be processed at one time; and much more.

Open order database access: Searchable by author, title, LCCN, ISBN, or a unique record number. Scrolling a summary of all MARC tags recognized by *MATSS* is possible.

Name:	**Orderit!**
Program type:	Acquisitions
Vendor:	Right On Programs
Cost:	$40
Hardware requirements:	Apple II series; Commodore 64; IBM PC, XT, PCjr.
Description:	This database system allows for input of publisher, title, author, and order date. Entries may be retrieved and sent to screen or printer by specific title or author. Menu options allow for listing all entries by publisher, author, or title. Operation, if RAM based, is quick and efficient. If mistake is made, however, it is not possible to correct it, short of deleting it and reentering. For small school library with limited needs, there is hardly any point to look further. This is all you need.
Documentation:	Self-documenting

Bibliography

Introduction

The production of bibliographies is important for many libraries. Some need "quick bibs," which consist of little more than the barest data—not in a rigorously standardized format, save that it is consistent. Other libraries require full bibliographies in a highly standardized format, with annotations. These bibliographies are often used as acquisition lists for the staff and public, catalogs, etc.

Of the many bibliography programs, two of them, *Personal Bibliographic System* and *Professional Bibliographic System*, are giants in their field and give users a wide range of options and capabilities, from a default standard of ANSI rules to customization with the user's rules. They also allow for downloading from such utilities as BRS, OCLC, and RLIN into the user's bibliographic format.

Another system, such as *Bibliography Writer* (Follett Software Company), is a less expensive bibliographic production program; it has less capability, but is easier to use.

Reviews

Bibliography Writer

Personal Bibliographic System

Pro-Cite

Professional Bibliographic System

Name: **Bibliography Writer**

Program type: Bibliography production

Vendor: Follett Software Company

Cost: $59.95

Hardware
requirements: Apple II series; TRS-80 Model III or IV

Capacity: The Apple offers 300 entries per disk without annotations, or 150 entries with annotations. The TRS-80 offers 500 entries, with annotations. Up to 7 bibliographies may be placed on a single disk.

Description: A solidly programmed package, *Bibliography Writer* provides an easy way to prepare and update professional-looking bibliographies. It is, however, rigidly inflexible, defining only seven fields: author (30 characters total), title (78), call number (12), city (20), publisher (25), copyright (4), and annotations up to 159 characters. Program is totally user friendly. After a brief startup for each bibliography, users may begin data entry with ease, and correct their mistakes with little difficulty. Bibliographies may be added to, deleted from, eliminated, or printed out.

Documentation: Sixteen-page booklet describes program operation, with special section for TRS-80 Model III users. Appended: Recovering disk space on the Apple; making copies with one or two Apple drives.

Name: **Personal Bibliographic System**

Program type: Bibliography production

Vendor: Personal Bibliographic Software, Inc.

Cost: $195 (separate versions must be purchased for Apple II+, IIe, or III). $75 for manual and demonstration package (may be applied to full package purchase)

Hardware
requirements: Apple II series, Apple III; 64K, two disk drives, 80-column display required for all versions

Description: Features include word processing, database management, text formatting, Boolean search capability, sort and print options. Data entry may use default form, or it may be customized. The system automatically formats for 20 document types: monographs (long and short), journals (long and short), reports, newspapers, dissertations, trade catalogs, letters, manuscripts, conference proceedings, maps, music scores, sound recordings, motion pictures, audiovisual material, video recordings, art works, computer programs, and data files. Wide range of printer control options includes manual sheet feed, margin width, line length, and more. Typical library uses include film catalogs, record and tape catalogs, new acquisition lists, archival holdings lists, reading lists, annotated lists of books, articles, filmstrips, etc. Uses American National Standard for Bibliographic Citations.

Although an excellent program with great capability, *Personal Bibliographic System* is not nearly as powerful as *Professional Bibliographic System* (reviewed below).

Documentation: Notebook has examples of completed bibliographies, as well as notes on systems special features and use.

Name: **Pro-Cite**

Program type: Bibliography production

Vendor: Personal Bibliographic Software, Inc.

Cost: $395 (sample disk $19.95; with manual, $75)

Hardware
requirements: IBM PC, XT, AT or M300

Capacity: 32,500 records per database

Description: Similar in many ways to *Professional Bibliographic System,* this enhanced and updated program provides much more power and capability. For instance, in addition to bibliography production, it allows for two user-designed workforms, full-text searching, unlimited keyword searches, full Boolean logic (including NOT), sort by any field (including "intelligent" data sorting), faster operation, and greater editing capabilities. Searching may be by any field or by specific field, with or without truncation, and by word, number, standardized date, workform type, or record number. Program uses ANSI as default for bibliographic style, simulates American Psychological (or Science) Association style, or users may construct their own style. Files may be saved to disk in standard ASCII format for further preparation with standard word processor. System may be used to import and reformat data from DIALOG, BRS, OCLC, and RLIN with corresponding *Biblio-Link* package ($195 each). Other features are online help file, variable length fields and records, detection of duplicate records (including immediate deletion option).

Documentation: Illustrated notebook describes the system and uses.

Name: **Professional Bibliographic System**

Program type: Bibliography production

Vendor: Personal Bibliographic Software, Inc.

Cost: $295 (Macintosh) and $395 (IBM versions). Cost of manual and demonstration of IBM version ($75) may be applied to full version if purchased later. Sample disk for Macintosh is $19.95.

Hardware requirements: IBM PC, XT, AT; M300; Macintosh (128K minimum RAM for all versions)

Capacity: Up to 1000 citations per floppy disk, to 32,500 per database

Description: This specialized database management, which produces professional-quality bibliographies, works well for course reading lists, acquisitions lists, book reviews, film catalogs, record and tape catalogs, archival holding lists, and anything for which bibliographic format is desired. Clearly the best standalone bibliographic system available today. Is menu driven, very easy to use, and has online help files. Program runs very fast, being Pascal based. American National Standard for Bibliographic References is default for punctuation and format, but users may create their own entry or punctuation format, and since standard ASCII files are generated, may further edit entries with almost any word processor. Entries may be searched rapidly, using abbreviated Boolean operators (e.g., A = And, O = Or). Wild card searching may be used on either right or left side of terms. Data entry takes 20 document types: monographs (short and long), journals (short and long), reports, newspapers, dissertations, trade catalogs, letters, manuscripts, conference proceedings, maps, music scores, sound recordings, motion pictures, audiovisual material, video recordings, art works, computer programs, and data files. Only desired fields need be printed out. To index a term, term must be stored in special index field (which holds up to 74 characters) at end of the record. Finished product may be sent to the printer or screen, or saved to disk.

System is flexible, supporting wide range of hardware and printer options. Records may be added manually or automatically from DIALOG, BRS, OCLC, or RLIN, or information may be imported from local databases (e.g., the library catalog) by adding *Biblio-Link*. This program is indispensable for extensive, professional-quality bibliography production.

Documentation: Looseleaf notebook has examples of finished products, listings of features, instructions, and special notes on using the system.

Related or
similar
programs: *Biblio-Link* ($195) allows downloaded files from OCLC, RLIN, BRS, or DIALOG (the last two only for Macintosh) to be formatted for use with *Professional Bibliographic System*

PC Dial ($25) is a dialup utility for users who do not have telecommunications or terminal software.

Additional
information: *Apple Library Users Group Newsletter,* January 1986, p. 16.

Cataloging

Introduction

Although many catalog card production programs are similar in design, purchasers should be aware of significant differences in cataloging rules, the ease with which entries may be corrected, whether cards may be stored for batch printing later, whether there is onscreen review of material exactly as it will be printed out (before it is printed), and whether a system will produce spine and book labels. A major problem in generating cards with a microcomputer is the fanfold catalog card paper; many printers will not take thick card stock or paper that has "microfine" perforations (i.e., perforations identical to those of noncomputer catalog cards after they have been separated). Some printers require special attachments to accept card stock.

Bibliofile, decidedly different from the other software in this category, provides in-house access to Library of Congress MARC bibliographic records for catalog production.

Sources of Additional Information

Shirinian, George. *"Catalog Card Maker"* (review), *Small Computers in Libraries,* February 1983, p. 5.

Tench, R. Terry. "Catalog Card Production Using *Applewriter,"* *Apple Library Users Group*, April 1985, p. 55.

Reviews

BiblioFile Catalog Production System

Card and Label Manager

Catalog Card and Label Writer 4.0

Catalog Card Maker III

Catalogit III
GRCComQuest
Librarian's Helper
Quick Card

Name: **BiblioFile Catalog Production System,** version 2.13

Program type: MARC bibliographic record files

Vendor: The Library Corporation

Cost: $2930, software and CD-ROM
$870, quarterly subscription to English MARC
$1470, monthly subscription to English MARC
$500, yearly subscription to Foreign MARC
Free disk-based demonstration available

Hardware
requirements: IBM PC, 256K, or M300

Used at: Chatham College
Pittsburgh Regional Library Center
Pittsburgh, PA 15232
Contact: David Wright
412-441-8200 ext. 220

Capacity: 3 million MARC records on four laser disks

Description: Provides in-house access to Library of Congress English-
and foreign-language MARC bibliographic records. The
four CD-ROM disks are periodically recompiled and
reissued, and system comes with CD-ROM player to at-
tach to user-supplied IBM PC. Functions include searching
the database, editing MARC records, creating original
MARC records, displaying catalog card image, saving
edited records, transmitting directly to another computer
system, printing cards and labels locally, and converting
to OCLC-type magnetic tape.
    Up to 99 titles may be recalled per search, and
search may be made by any word in title, author's name,
ISBN, or LCCN. Items may be saved to disk, which may
be searched later to review work. Printer options allow
for customization of cards. Program will also print spine

or book pocket labels. Help windows are available at any time and easy to summon and use.

Program was used successfully to expedite retrospective conversion by Phillips Memorial Library, Providence College (see citation below), which has 250,000 volumes, 110,000 of which were converted to machine-readable form. If a MARC record was found in *BiblioFile* database, it was stored on a floppy disk for later editing and, ultimately, stored in library's catalog.

Documentation: Unknown

Additional
information: Desmarais, Norman. *"BiblioFile," Library Software Review*, January–February 1986, p. 28.

Desmarais, Norman. *"BiblioFile* for Retrospective Conversion," *Small Computers in Libraries,* December 1985, p. 24.

Name: **Card and Label Manager**

Program type: Catalog card production

Vendor: Speak Softly, Inc.

Cost: $169 Apple II+; $199 Apple IIe
$249 IBM PC
$100 Booklist (sort) option

Hardware
requirements: Apple II+, two disk drives; Apple IIe or IIc, one or two disk drives, 80-column card; IBM PC, one or two disk drives, DOS 1.1 or later. Printers are Okidata, Epson, Apple, NEC, Prowriter, Letter Quality. Program will work with other printers if "other" option is selected.

Description: From a single entry, this program prints catalog card sets, labels for book pockets, circulation cards, and spine labels in three formats. System comes configured for standard format, and if that meets library's needs, program may be running in minutes. Master Menu displays five choices: Enter new data, Edit/review existing data, Print or test print, Utilities, and Exit. From Utility menu, data disk may be initialized, hardware specifications changed, and other decisions made. Booklist or sort option may be installed in Utilities.

Documentation: Program has 50-page manual with many examples, as well as notes on hardware configuration, a step-by-step tutorial on entire system, and additional notes on printers and disk care.

Name: **Catalog Card and Label Writer,** 4.0

Program type: Catalog card production

Vendor: K–12 MicroMedia Publishing

Cost: $169; $199 Apple II+ with lowercase adapter

Hardware requirements: Apple II series; IBM; TRS-80 III, IV; Commodore 64. Printer card must be in slot 1. System will configure for serial or parallel printers. Demonstrator version will store only two labels and print its own description on your catalog card entries.

Capacity: Cards must be printed out immediately; only label information may be saved for later printing.

Description: Program automates typing of catalog cards, labels for book spines, checkout cards, and pockets. If material is too lengthy to fit onto card, second card is automatically generated. Cards must be printed immediately, since only label information is stored on disk. Labels are printed separately later, allowing card stock in printer to be changed conveniently. Label information stored on disk remains in system until separate program, *Label Deleter* (included), is used. Not possible to create catalog of materials with this program.

System allows entry of 14 items (each followed by maximum allowable characters per entry): type of media (10), title of book (56), joint author/editor/illustrator (66), author (36), publisher (56), copyright date (26), collation (33), description (150), book call number (8), book call letters (8), purchase source (25), book purchase price (6), added entries (total of 5 added entries allowed), subjects (combined total of 8 added entries/subjects allowable and combined total of 232 characters). Once everything has been entered, users can make corrections. Label sets may be printed to maximum of 30 labels per set. Possible to store label information for 75 to 100 titles before it becomes necessary to print labels.

Additional
information: Bjorner, Susan N. "Catalog Card Production: A Comparison of Two Software Packages," *Small Computers in Libraries,* July 1982, p. 1.

Documentation: Eighteen-page booklet with description, full instructions, sample cards (author, title, subject, shelf cards), and sample labels

Name: **Catalog Card Maker III,** version 1.4

Program type: Catalog card production

Vendor: Winnebago Software Co.

Cost: $149

Hardware
requirements: Apple II series (48K) with 80-column printer, one disk drive

Capacity: 400 cards may be saved for later batch printing, or 1500 labels.

Description: Several advanced features come with this package, including ability to save records as they are entered for later batch printing of cards and labels. Cards may be printed according to either AACR2 or traditional style (pre-AACR2). Users also control whether complete card set is printed or only main card, as well as height of card, width, gap between cards, and margin. All these features come in default mode, ready for continuous card stock. Printer slot is selectable, and will also make labels. Four predetermined label formats come with system, but customized version may be created.

Documentation: Thirty-seven–page booklet is complete, with instructions for setting card specifications and for making printer adjustments, printing labels, and copying data diskettes.

Name: **Catalogit III**

Program type: Card catalog production

Vendor: Right On Programs

Cost: $75

Hardware
requirements: Apple II series; IBM PC, PCjr., XT

Capacity: Ten card sets may be saved for later batch printing

Description: Like other Right On programs, this is extremely user friendly, allowing data entry to begin immediately. In fact, only three options on main menu: enter data, print cards, quit. Included are 500 continuous feed cards, so there's no need to wait for supplies. Program follows AACR2 cataloging rules. Up to 10 card sets may be stored before it is necessary to print, thus saving time.

  With this updated version, it is possible to preview cards on screen before printing. Special insert mode makes it easy to update cards without retyping whole line or entry. Records contain call number (3 lines of 8 characters each); author, title, publisher information (edition, publishing city, publishing house); copyright date; up to four subject headings; illustrations; book description (number of pages, drawings, maps, etc.); illustrator; and annotations. Cards may be printed as individual book cards for author (2 per set), title, editor, joint author, illustrator, or up to four subject cards—or program will produce complete card set automatically.

  The Apple version I inspected did not allow typing quite as fast as desired. Once the person who enters data adjusts to slight drop in speed, there should be little difficulty.

Documentation: Fifteen-page booklet with complete instructions.

Name: **GRCComQuest**

Program type: Retrospective conversion

Vendor: General Research Corporation

Cost: Consult vendor

Hardware
requirements: IBM PC, IBM compatibles, or M300. One disk drive and
256K required. Hayes Smartmodem 1200 or equivalent

Description: Program designed for facilitating library's retrospective
conversion (converts records to MARC II format) at up
to 500 per hour. Each transaction is entered locally, then
matched against GRCCOM database at 1200 baud. Full
MARC records (6 LC-defined formats) are returned to
library on magnetic tape or establish database for producing COM catalog. Update section allows for continued
editing and maintenance of database, including Field
Updates, Record Updates, Indicator Changes, Subfield
Changes, Branch Changes, Authority Control Updates,
and Cross Reference Updates. Original Entry section
allows for original cataloging for books, visual materials,
archival and manuscript control, geography and maps,
music, and serials.

Documentation: Consult vendor

Related
programs: *LaserQuest* (General Research Corporation) is a compact
laser disk system, containing over 4 million MARC
records.

Name: **Librarian's Helper: Productivity Tool for Librarians,**
version 4.0

Program type: Catalog card production

Vendor: Scarecrow Press, Inc.

Cost: $325, Apple II/IIe (includes CP/M card)
$225, IBM PC and compatibles
$10, demonstration
$30, updates

Hardware
requirements: Apple II/IIe (64K); IBM PC (256K). Printers: Prowriter,
Epson, IBM Graphics, and others.
        Apple version requires 80 columns. Two disk drives
required for "save" feature. MS-DOS (2.0 or up), PC-DOS,
CP/M, or CP/M-86

Capacity: Ten added entries, 10 subjects, 5 lines for call numbers

Description: Complete cataloging package provides for multiple card sets, onscreen viewing, and saving material to disk for bibliography or database production, all according to AACR2 cataloging rules. Thirty-two data fields available, any of which may be eliminated from data entry routine if they are not needed. Program is menu-driven, and information is fed in at prompts. Program provides easy editing of records at any point. Custom configuration available if proper information is given to Scarecrow Press when order is placed. Special "save" feature, available for additional charge, permits records to be saved to disk for later printing, and to print out information as a bibliography sorted by author, title, or call number. Data may even be transferred from disk to online catalogs and database programs. Several new features added to version 4.0, including *Backup,* which allows editing previous entries; diagnostic and repair program, which will recover damaged files; data security routine; and improved sort time. With Apple version I used, it was not possible to print a single card at a time; it prints a whole set or nothing.

Documentation: Program comes with 30 pages of documentation in small looseleaf binder. Includes several sources for card stock and other supplies necessary to use *Librarian's Helper.* Akers's *Simple Library Cataloging* (7th ed., Scarecrow) by Arthur Curley and Jana Varlejs, is included.

Additional
information: "Software Review: *Librarian's Helper,*" *Kansas Library Automation News,* March 1985, p. 23

Name: **Quick Card**

Program type: Catalog card production

Vendor: Follett Software Company

Cost: $169.95 Apple II; $249.95 IBM PC

Hardware
requirements: Apple II series; IBM PC

Capacity: See below

Description: Menu-driven, easy-to-use, fill-in-the-blanks program
follows AACR2 cataloging rules, as well as Dewey or LC
classification systems. Prints card or label sets, or proof
sheets. Record fields are classification (8 lines of 8
characters each), author (80), title (150), responsibility
(80), edition (80), physical descriptions (80), series (80),
materials (80), publications (120); and subject headings,
added entries, and analytics have six fields of 80 characters
each. (Difficult to imagine anything left out of data fields.)

All fields may be permanently "enabled" or
"disabled," as desired, to conform to particular library's
needs. Changing parameters is quick. Card is seen on
screen as it will be printed on paper, and changes are easily
made. Both margins and spacing between cards on continuous stock may be specified. Pitch or characters per
inch may be specified as pica or elite. When card set is
printed out, only desired cards may be "enabled." Once
batch of cards has been entered, all cards or range of cards
may be printed out. Labels may be printed out three across.

Additional
information: Anderson, Eric S. "Quick Card" (a review), *Apple Library
Users Group Newsletter,* April 1985, p. 33

Documentation: Forty-page booklet has numerous tutorials on operation:
getting started, setting card fields, adding cards, deleting
cards, printing card/label sets, and making new data disk.
Appendix A: "Making Copies on the Apple with One Disk
Drive," "Making Copies on the Apple with Two Disk
Drives"; Appendix B: "Making Copies on the IBM PC"

Children's Services/Library Skills

Introduction

In addition to administrative work, some of the "traditional" library activities associated with children may be automated. These include the formerly laborious job of producing word puzzles, or the thankless (not to mention, endless) task of teaching library skills. To aid the librarian who wishes to determine readability calculations for various types of printed materials, automated programs exist for that as well.

Other software will keep track of kids' reading during the summer reading club. Some of the database or word processing materials presented in other chapters may also be used to maintain reading club scores or records and to produce handouts, flyers, and press releases.

The software in this section will

Generate specialized reading lists for teachers, students, or patrons
Gauge reading levels of written materials
Assist library instruction
Create puzzles (word find, crossword, etc.)
Test reading materials
Track reading club participation

Reviews

Almanacs

Bartlett's Familiar Quotations

Crossword Magic

Electronic Bookshelf

Electronic Library Media Skills

Puzzles and Posters

Readability Calculations

Ripley's Library Research Skills

Skills Maker

Using an Index to Periodicals

Name:	**Almanacs**
Program type:	Library skills
Vendor:	Calico
Cost:	$25
Hardware Requirements:	Apple II series
Grade level:	3 to 6
Description:	Introduces students to use of different types of almanacs. Thirty-six pages (screens) allow both forward movement and/or review of any page at any time. Multiple-choice and scramble puzzles, used throughout, make program interactive and enhance learning, and positive reinforcement boosts learners' morale. Projects for further study are listed at end of program.
Documentation:	Self-documenting
Related programs:	Calico also offers library instruction modules, including *Bartlett's Familiar Quotations* (reviewed below), *Poetry Indexes,* and *Periodical Indexes.*

Name:	**Bartlett's Familiar Quotations**
Program type:	Library skills
Vendor:	Calico
Cost:	$25

Hardware
requirements: Apple II series

Description: This delightful program gives good instruction on 14th and
15th editions of *Bartlett's.* Material is presented in 36 pages
(screens) of explanatory text and multiple-choice questions. Students may flip to any page *from* any page, making review quick and easy. No negative aspects to learning
situation, just positive reinforcement. Material is divided
into description of *Bartlett's,* hints on its use, how it is indexed, and special section on 15th edition. If student
answers enough questions, gets free ride on "Bartlett's
Balloon."

Grade level: 3 through 6

Documentation: Self-documenting

Name: **Crossword Magic**

Vendor: Mindscape, Inc.

Cost: $49.95 (includes backup disk)

Hardware
requirements: Apple II series, Apple III; Atari; Commodore 64; IBM.
Printer recommended (works with numerous dot matrix
printers)

Used at: Liverpool Public Library
Second and Tulip Sts.
Liverpool, NY 13088
315-457-0310

Grade level: 2 and up

Description: Automates production of crossword puzzles, just as
Puzzles and Posters (described below) automates production of word-find puzzles. There are differences,
however. *Crossword Magic,* while simple to operate, is
not as straightforward as *Puzzles and Posters.* For a word-
find puzzle, it is necessary only to enter a wordlist, then
wait a few moments for puzzle to be printed. With
Crossword Magic, a more active role is necessary, since
a crossword puzzle requires not only wordlist but clues

as well. This product will not make perfect puzzles all by itself (i.e., they will not look like newspaper puzzles) from randomly selected words, since unlike a crossword puzzle, the spaces between words in a word-find are filled in with random letters. Planning and editing, in (M)anual mode, are therefore necessary to "dress it up."

Puzzles, though they will not look exactly like those in a newspaper, are excellent, and working with the program is fun, in the same way solving a crossword puzzle is fun—just backward. Program creates puzzle so many squares wide or down, if specified (smallest is 3 × 3), or expands grid to accommodate all words as they are entered. Program holds unused words (words that won't fit) in special buffer, where they remain until they fit, when they pop out to expand the puzzle dramatically. Puzzles may be 3 to 20 boxes across and down. Best to make list of words on paper first, especially if topical puzzle is being created. Feed in most important or longest words first, and fit the last words manually (if necessary). Puzzles may have 80 or more words, or as few as desired, and may be saved to disk and edited later. Making a puzzle takes 30 minutes (at most). One demonstration puzzle is included. Sound may be turned off.

Documentation: Program comes with two booklets: operating manual (23 pages of start-up information, instructions, method for creating good puzzles, and tips) and teacher's manual (24 pages, which contains 7 reproducible sample puzzles with clues).

Name: **Electronic Bookshelf**

Program type: Specialized database management system

Vendor: The Electronic Bookshelf, Inc.

Cost: $115 for program disk and documentation with backup
$35 for each title disk with backup
"Lab Paks" are $175 for 5 program disks and 1 documentation
$250 for 10 program disks and 1 documentation
$70 for 5 title disks of same volume
$135 for 10 titles disks of same volume

Hardware
requirements: Apple II series, 64K

Grade level: Series I, 3–6; series II, 5–9; series III, 8–12

Description: Program is easy to use, providing quick-quiz material for more than 500 popular titles in three grade levels. Scores are recorded on disk, which makes it easy to see who's been reading and how well they've done during summer program or with class assignments. Quiz questions are randomly selected for each test. Customized quiz questions and answers may be entered by librarian or teacher, and are rated by difficulty. Operation by young people is easy. Anyone who uses it, however, must have "group" disk, which must be prepared by teacher or librarian, but many students may use the same disk. Each quiz has 5 to 10 questions (this and other options are "open" to person in charge of program), all multiple choice.

Sample of books in series I is *Anything for a Friend; Summer to Die; Tiger Eyes; Black Stallion; Lion, Witch, and Wardrobe;* and *Twenty-one Balloons.* Series II: *Accident; Letter Perfect; Snow Bound; Tarzan of the Apes; Yearling; Dragonquest; Swiss Family Robinson; Sea Wolf; Candy Man; Durango Street;* and *Prince Caspian.* Series III: *Adventures of Tom Sawyer; Alas Babylon; Cheaper by the Dozen; Death of a Salesman; Nineteen Eighty-four; Separate Peace; Raisin in the Sun; Ox Bow Incident;* and *Flowers for Algernon.*

Documentation: Sixty-page manual, indexed, filled with tips for proper use of program. Complete start-up information, including how to copy backups.

Name: **Elementary Library Media Skills**

Program type: Library skills

Vendor: Combase, Inc.

Cost: $125 per module, $350 complete set

Grade level: 3 to 6 and adult

Hardware
requirements: Apple II series

Description: Most comprehensive micro-based library instruction set available, in four modules (12 disks):

1. *Discovering Available Resources*
   Media Resources
   Media Classifications
   [fiction, nonfiction, biography]
2. *Locating Resources*
   Card Catalog
   [alphabetical order, author, title and subject cards, bibliographic information]
   Locating Materials
   [guide letters and words, call numbers]
3. *Organization of Resources*
   Alphabetical Order
   [author names, subject headings, book titles]
   Numerical Order
   [3-place numbers, decimal numbers, numbers and letters]
   Biographical Order
   [biographies]
4. *Research and Study Skills*
   Basic Reference Skills
   [reference tools, dictionary, encyclopedia, atlas]
   Research Skills
   [finding information, writing reports]

Highly interactive program makes good use of graphics, puzzles, and riddles, and is generally entertaining. Students select specific area for study or (literally) take entire course in library skills. Lessons are straightforward, requiring no special knowledge or understanding of computers, and programs are self-paced, allowing students to stop to reflect at any point or go back to previous page or pages. "Mickey Micro," a whimsical screen character, provides positive reinforcement. Each lesson begins with quick overview of material to be learned. *Fiction* module, for example, allows students to pick separate lessons ("What Is Fiction?" "Call Numbers for Fiction," and "Call Number Game [for Fiction]"). Thirty-day return privilege.

Documentation:	Reproducible worksheets in massive notebook, as well as list of educational objectives and suggestions for further learning and activities.
Name:	**Puzzles and Posters**
Program type:	Graphics and puzzles production
Vendor:	MECC
Hardware requirements:	Apple (64K); IBM PC (128K); Commodore 64; TRS-80 III/IV; Atari (48K)
Cost:	$59, Apple II series, 64K $49, IBM, 128K; Commodore 64; TRS-80 III/IV $39, Atari, 48K, including backups
Grade level:	1 to adult
Description:	Word puzzles, on any theme and in various sizes, can be created in a few minutes. Disk contains four programs: "Word Search," "Crossword Puzzle," "A-maze-ment," and "Posters and Banners." Word puzzles created in three simple steps: (1) Choose set of words; (2) enter them at keyboard, as prompted by computer (up to 50-word-list, or 15 characters each, may be created for temporary use or permanently stored on data disk); and (3) computer creates the puzzle. At this point, either stencil or spirit master may be used. Program also generates answer sheet.

Clip art or other illustrations can be added to produce camera-ready copy for photo offset. Since program eliminates drudgery associated with creating such puzzles, puzzles may be created for almost any occasion (or to enliven a library newsletter). Puzzle flyers can be used as seasonal handouts—for Christmas, Halloween, spring, winter, fall, etc. ("Summer Fun!" "Dieter's Delight!" "Monsters of the World!" "Library Fun!"). "A-maze-ment," an interesting feature not found with other puzzle or game programs, is Apple exclusive, and Apple dot matrix printer is used; text version (not impressive) is printed on other printers. Smallest puzzle is 3 × 3 characters; largest is 23 × 25.

Crossword puzzle component does not have nearly the power or flexibility of *Crossword Magic* (also reviewed in this volume), but it produces a crossword puzzle. If

Imagewriter printer is used, crossword puzzle looks good. Printouts from other printers are not as elegant, and should be used only as pattern for creating final puzzle. Posters and banners may be printed, but program has neither the clip art, flexibility, nor quality of *The Print Shop*.

Documentation: Program's 36-page looseleaf binder has complete instructions, illustrations, and examples of completed work (and screenshots).

Name: **Readability Calculations**

Program type: Text analysis

Vendor: Micro Power & Light Co.

Cost: $49, IBM; $44, Apple II

Hardware requirements: IBM PC, XT, PCjr. (128K with DOD 2.0, 64K with DOS 1.0); Apple II series

Description: Program will calculate text reading level according to nine formulas. Just type in part of manuscript, novel, textbook, or other reading material and computer returns a screenful of data. IBM version will analyze files created with word processor, making it easy to spot-check user's manuscript, whether from curiosity or to ascertain proper level. Formulas are Dale-Chall, Fry, Flesch, Flesch-Kincaid, Fog, Ari, Coleman, Powers, Holmquist. Excellent program for recommending or using particular text. This program could easily be in word processing section of this book as a writing aid, like a spelling program or electronic thesaurus.

Documentation: Twenty-eight–page manual describes various tests and has overview for starting, tutorial, and bibliography for further reading.

Name: **Ripley's Library Research Skills**

Program type: Library skills/multimedia set

Vendor: Society for Visual Education, Inc.

Cost: $219, software, filmstrips, tapes
$79, software only
$20, backups

Hardware
requirements: Apple II series, 48K

Grade level: 4–6, 7 and 8 remediation

Description: To make full use of this excellent multimedia set, this package needs (besides microcomputer) filmstrip projector and cassette tape player. The tapes ("Exploring the Library with Ripley's," "Starting Your Research on Ripley's," "Ripley's Introduces Other Sources," and "Confirming Your Ripley's Research") go with the four filmstrips. The two diskettes (4 sides) are for beginners and advanced students ("Ripley's Beginning Library Research Skills" and beginning and advanced "Ripley's Using Other Library Sources"). Diskette programs are combination of quiz, game, and rewards. Object is to proceed through library (represented as game board) by answering questions about encyclopedias, almanacs, atlases, and other reference tools.

Everything is well done. Print is large and easy to read; catalog cards are displayed on screen for some exercises, allowing students to find call number, author, publisher, etc., for points. "Ripley fact" is displayed every question or two to maintain interest and give reinforcement for correct answers. Some "facts" are animated (a wink or wave, etc., from Ripley character). Other graphics include set of encyclopedias and card catalog, represented on screen. Student must pick proper volume or drawer to answer a question correctly. System's disk management allows teacher to keep track of student's performance, as well as "save" student's place so he or she need not start at the beginning after a break.

Comes with complete set of catalog cards and labels. Comprehensive filmstrips include material about almanac, atlas, autobiography, bibliography, biography, call number, card catalog, classification system, dictionary, encyclopedia, fiction, index, nonfiction, periodicals, plagiarism, research topic, table of contents, title page, working list, and vertical file. Material and presentation are excellent, using color, interesting graphics, and logic to impart basic understanding of library skills. Each filmstrip has 50–57 frames, and script for each filmstrip is given in accompanying guide. All materials are packaged in convenient binder.

Documentation: Manual has many reproducible worksheets for the four filmstrips.

Name: **Skills Maker**

Program type: Library instruction authoring system

Vendor: Follett Software Company

Cost: $89.95

Hardware requirements: Apple II series, printer

Description: One of new generation of library "do it" programs; that is, students go to shelves to answer questions posed by computer. It is an authoring system for producing printed exercises, not a hands-on program for students. Program can be customized for particular library (which assures that books are actually owned by library). Books include *Readers' Guide* (part 1 teaches author and subject entries; part 2, *see* and *see also*), almanacs, dictionaries, atlases, and encyclopedias.

Review source: *Apple Library Users Group Newsletter,* December 1984, p. 22

Name: **Using an Index to Periodicals**

Program type: Library skills

Vendor: Combase, Inc.

Cost: $50 for each of two levels

Hardware requirements: Apple II series, 48K

Grade level: 6–9 and adult

Description: Microcomputer-based introduction to *Readers' Guide to Periodical Literature* on elementary and advanced levels. Both contain introduction to information indexes, including interactive tutorial on differences between card catalog, magazine index, and back-of-book index. Level 1 has tutorials on organization of *Readers' Guide,* on its use, on special features, and a checkout test. For most part, the two levels cover the same ground, but level 2 is slightly higher (for someone who is acquainted with *Readers' Guide*). Level 2 has checklist instead of test. Good interaction and graphics throughout. Program is self-documenting. Completion time is 30 to 60 minutes.

Documentation: Reproducible worksheets for program include facsimile pages from *Readers' Guide,* self-tests, and research exercise accompanies each package.

Review Source: *Apple Library Users Group Newsletter,* April 1985, p. 32

Circulation

Introduction

Several software packages in this section are complete circulation systems for small libraries (e.g., elementary, high school, and very small public libraries). These packages usually require a hard disk, and contain acquisitions, overdues, circulation, and other components and modules. They are, in a sense, integrated software packages for library circulation and acquisitions.

A single function package such as *Reserve Power* allows libraries to take advantage of automation without a great investment in money or time. A library which has a special department for lending films, or a high school media center which attempts to keep track of where its films are supposed to be, may invest in a software package which will do that and only that.

Again, as has been stressed throughout this book, many libraries have taken general software, such as *AppleWorks,* and applied it to a host of library applications.

Sources of Additional Information

Bahnmiller, Dave. "Using a Microcomputer to Control a Paperback Collection," *Apple Library Users Group Newsletter,* October 1985, p. 52.
Cybulski, JoAnne. "Periodical Management with Appleworks," *Apple Library Users Group Newsletter,* July 1985, p. 29.

Reviews

Book Trak I

Circulation Manager

Circulation Plus

Library Circulation System I/II/III

Reserve Power

Name: **Book Trak I: Hard Disk Circulation System**

Program Type: Circulation system

Vendor: Richmond Software Corporation

Cost: $850 (includes Barcode Label Printing Program). Richmond also sells all peripheral hardware, including 10, 20, or 30 MB drives, controller cards, clock cards, and Barwand. Demonstration disk available (contact vendor)

Hardware
requirements: Apple IIe, 128K; 80-column extended text card, ProDOS-compatible hard disk, clock card, Barwand, printer (contact Richmond for list)

Capacity: 3000 to 250,000 collection (depending upon disk space)

Description: Menu-driven program uses barcode scanner and fast "pop-up" windows so often seen with ProDOS programs. Data entry fields are bar code number, author (42 characters), call number (42), title (70), ISBN, LC number, subject (30), location/status (30), loan period. Patrons data entry includes bar code number, name (25), street address (24), city (30), state (30), zip code (10), phone number (10), grade (30), homeroom (30), borrowing period for individual, card expiration date, and graduation year (2). Ideal for school libraries. Patrons may be searched by name, city, state, zip code, grade, or homeroom. Item may be searched by author, call number, title, ISBN, and LC number. Patrons may borrow up to 15 items and make 3 reserves.

Documentation: Manual was being revised as this was written, but mockup we were permitted to see contained several hundred pages and covered all operations.

Name: **Circulation Manager**

Program type: Circulation system

Vendor: Professional Software

Cost: $350

Hardware
requirements: IBM PC, XT, or AT, 256K; one floppy disk, 132-column printer

Capacity: Program intended for libraries that have 100–400 items in circulation at one time and active patron list to 700

Description: Intended for special library, such as hospital. To make this system work, it is necessary to set up patron, circulation, and miscellany files, which may be done with relative ease (especially considering small number of patrons). Program menus are clear and easy to follow, and program executes swiftly. It is also necessary to set up system with specific data on lending rules, printer parameters, and form-letter templates (overdues, reserves, expiration notices).

    Form-letter function is remarkable: users may input their own overdue notice, reserve letter, etc., with built-in text editor. Circulation file contains call number, author (optional), title, start and due dates of loan; and links to four categories of material are allowed: journal, audiovisual, other, and "none of the above" (book). Items may be retrieved by call number, author's last name (or string), title (or string), and Boolean operator AND. Separate loan and renewal periods may be established for each category, and nine patron categories are supported. Parameters for mailing labels may be specified by lines, columns, or labels across the page. Ideal for small special libraries, where no lengthy data entry process is desired.

Documentation: Excellent thumb-indexed, looseleaf binder covers all important areas in detail, including installation, keyboard control, reports, check-in/check-out, statistics, etc. Appended are "Special Keys" and sample printouts: patron file, current circulation (call number and patron), overdue items, items on reserve, items held by patrons whose privileges soon expire, circulation statistics, and form letters for overdues, reserve notices, and patrons who are leaving the institution. Index.

Name: **Circulation Plus**

Program type: Circulation system

Vendor: Follett Software Co.

Cost: $695
                  $945 with scanner
                  $495 upgrade from Book Trak

$250 Barcode scanner

Apple IIe or IBM PC demonstrator free with manual on disk; with bound manual, $25

Hardware requirements:

Apple IIe with 80-column printer, two floppy disk drives, 80-column card, 5 or 10 megabyte profile disk drive; TRS-80 III or IV, 48K, two drives, 5 megabyte, 80-column printer; IBM PC AT, XT; Tandy 1200 (1 floppy drive and hard disk), game control adapter card, and 80-column printer

Capacity:

Patrons, 8000 (5MB), 15,000 (10MB IBM)

Books, 30,000 (5MB), 65,000 (10MB IBM)

Description:

This circulation system for small public or school libraries allows reserve, renewal, and fine records; prints overdue notices, bills, and reserve notices; and uses bar code for data entry during check-out. Patron status is checked automatically for overdues, fines, etc. Circulation statistics are generated for quick reports. Multiple due dates permitted. Speed of this program is exceptional, requiring maximum 5 seconds to complete a search. Floppy drives back up data from the hard disk.

May take a long time to get this system running since books must be bar coded and bibliographic data entered, either all at once (in the beginning) or gradually, as books are checked out. When a book is checked out, machine-readable label is applied on the book and another on the card, which is then set aside for later entry. Password system prevents unauthorized entries.

Fields in patron records are name (20 characters last name, 10 characters first name), special location (such as homeroom or teacher's name (15), street address (20), city (15), state (2), zip code (10), patron card number (12), phone number (3, 7), card expiration date (5), school year (2), type of patron (1). Some of these fields may be set up as default values (especially useful if most patrons live in same city or area code). Program also permits correction of one field at a time before leaving Add/Update section. Books may use the following fields: title (50 characters), author/call number (20), price (6), four circulation periods (1), categories 1 and 2 (3 digits each).

Statistical reports may include Dewey numbers, as

well as categories 1 and 2 (above), which allow for arbitrary assignment of numbers for special codes (e.g., "4" may equal a special fund). Circulation statistics on these books may be pulled later.

Program is quite sophisticated. For example, from the check-out screen, books or patron names may be searched directly to determine status; names may be searched by partial match; books may be renewed with a keystroke; books may be reserved or due date reassigned. System will print notices for overdue expired cards, reserves, or bills for mailing (if patrons' addresses have been entered). Will also print list of patrons who owe money, or whose cards have expired, and complete title or patron list. Other reports include collection breakdown by Dewey divisions, other categories, or free bar codes. Option allows inventory on separate computer, using only floppy drives. Books are inventoried by barcode scanner on movable computer cart.

Documentation: Manual, which may be printed from demonstration disk or purchased as hardcopy for $25, has several tutorials and screenshots, as well as separate sections on book checkout/renewal and check-in, add/update options, print/display options, system setup options, inventory options, and backup/quit. Depending upon printer, manual is printed from demonstration disk in 30 to 60 minutes.

Name: **Library Circulation System I/II/III**

Program type: Circulation system

Vendor: Winnebago Software Co.

Cost: *I*, $675
II, $895 ($1144.95 with metal bar code)
III (hard disk version), $995 ($1244.95 with metal bar wand)

Hardware
requirements: Apple II series, 64K, two disk drives, Epson printer (MX-80, MX-100, FX-100) with Graftrax 80, or Apple dot matrix, or NEC PC-8023 A-C dot matrix, or Apple Imagewriter DMP, bar code wand

Capacity: See below

Description: This series of three programs, each increasingly sophisticated, is intended for school libraries, though very small public libraries (whose patron base and book collection are small) may also use it. Can generate physical inventory (all material and equipment), analysis of circulation statistics for collection development, list of "out" material in a certain topic (as well as material checked out by a particular student), and daily and annual circulation figures. Overdue items are flagged and overdue list is automatically printed. All three versions use bar code wand.

As with other bar code systems, labels must be applied to all circulated items. Other preliminary figuring is required as well, such as reserving ample space on each disk. All acquisitions may be added to highest-number disk or space may be reserved on any disk for new acquisitions, but each disk may be sorted only within itself. Despite number of diskettes which may be involved, it is not necessary to change diskettes during circulation.

Library Circulation System I ($695), for small library, will accommodate 19,000 materials. Includes functions of circulation, overdues, inventory, and label printing, and plastic bar wand.

Library Circulation System II will accommodate 3500 user names, 60,000 items, 1000 reserves.

Library Circulation System III uses Corvus hard disk, eliminating need for diskettes except as backups, and handles up to 5000 users, 60,000 items, and 1000 reserves.

Documentation: Manual (approximately 100 pages) has general instructions; examples; glossary; setup and data entry procedures; how-to sections for overdues, printing lists of users and materials, printing bar code labels, and printing other lists (such as overdues or overdue notices, usage by type of material, etc.); circulation procedures; taking inventory; and helpful hints and tips.

Name: **Reserve Power**

Program type: Film and media reserves

Vendor:	Swan Software
Cost:	$750 $50, demonstration package $4, shipping and handling $150, annotation module $150, remote access module
Hardware requirements:	Apple IIe with 80c and 128K; IBM PC, XT, or compatible. Minimum 5 megabyte hard disk drive for all configurations. System will also work with Apple 3.5-inch Unidisk.
Capacity:	32,000 titles, patrons, and reservations
Description:	Excellent program for schools or media centers that lend substantial number of items. Materials such as films, videotapes, filmstrips—or just about any other audiovisual—may be entered into this calendar system and retrieved. Reports may be generated in eight ways, including lists, cross-referenced catalog, reservation slips, statistical studies, and inventory checklist. Materials may be searched by title, patron name, or by call number, category, or subject; and may be classified under 32 main categories, with up to 32 cross-referenced subjects in each category. However, *Reserve Power* has full-year calendar that permits any material to be reserved up to one year. For example, when a title is retrieved, a full-year calendar for that item appears on the screen, which will tell when item will be in use and to whom it is scheduled for loan. Other important data, such as run time, date in/out, YTD RES, call number, status ("available/not available"), and YTD CANCEL, may be added. Additional modules supply annotations for all materials or remotely access and alter the database.
Documentation:	Package comes with looseleaf binder of detailed instructions and examples of printed reports. Of special interest are five appendixes for help with error messages; suggested daily, monthly, and yearly schedules; and suggestions on how to increase storage capacity.

Communications and Online Database Systems (Including Electronic Bulletin Boards)

Introduction

Chief among the many useful functions that programs in this chapter perform is improving the way in which users connect to an online system or database such as Dialog, BRS, The Source, CompuServe, or any other utility. They may also connect to something as humble as an electronic bulletin board system (BBS), or some of the programs allow libraries to set up their own BBS. Some bulletin boards are operated by librarians for the public, while others expedite interlibrary loans. (See references below for setting up your own BBS.)

Beyond saving the trouble of dialing the digits manually, these programs provide many additional services: downloading (saving) material, uploading material prepared offline (when a database is not connected to another computer—as opposed to online, when contact with a remote database has been made) to another computer or system (such as an electronic mail network), which saves both time and money since it reduces online time. Some systems provide an online thesaurus to aid in selection of a database. They usually provide easy control of many functions associated with telecommunications as well, such as turning a printer on or off, setting baud or duplex boundaries, activating macros (automatic typing or executing a predetermined group of commands as if they were typed in at the keyboard). Some systems contain a word processor online (though these are generally primitive line editors). The list is almost endless.

Another exciting online service is provided by *MICROsearch* and *Search Helper*: both let patrons log onto a database service (without the aid of a librarian) and perform a search. (These are known as "gateway" services.) A somewhat similar database service is the ERIC local search system, which allows access to the ERIC database on disk.

Sources of Additional Information

Barrett, Judy. *Joys of Computer Networking.* McGraw-Hill, 1984.

Beeston, Tom, and Tom Tucker. *Hooking In: The Underground Computer* (Bulletin Board Workbook and Guide). Computer Food Press, 1983.

Cane, Mike. *The Computer Phone Book.* Plume, 1986 (1623 Broadway, New York, NY 10019).

Dewey, Patrick R. "Dear ABBS: Marketing, Maintenance and Suggestions," *Small Computers in Libraries,* September 1982, p. 1.

Glossbrenner, Alfred. *The Complete Handbook of Personal Computer Communications.* St. Martin's Press, 1985.

Stone, M. David. *Getting Online.* Prentice-Hall, 1984.

Library Software Review (November–December 1985) published five articles on use of the BBS by special and public libraries.

Reviews

ACCESS Microcomputer Network System

ASCII Express

BBS–PC

EasyNet

GBBS

MICROsearch

PC/NET LINK

People's Message System

Pro-Search

Search Helper

Smartcom I/II

Name:	**ACCESS Microcomputer Network System**
Program type:	Electronic mail
Vendor:	Information Intelligence, Inc.

Cost: $250, main program (quantity discounts)
$25, add-on auxiliary file program
$25, add-on system name (allows user to change system name)
$25, add-on module for message autodelete

Hardware requirements: Apple II+ or IIe, 48K, DOS 3.3; Hayes or Hayes-compatible, Apple, Novation Apple CAT III, and other modems; two disk drives; clock card; system does not support hard drive.

Description: Excellent package for Apple owners who want to set up electronic bulletin board system for professional networking. Program does not have some features or power which come with basic package of *People's Message System* (PMS, below), but has many other good features (some must be purchased separately) which make it attractive for interlibrary loan or library networking. Features include five levels of security passwords; automatic log on; online help; user-designed, automatic form fill-out (survey) (messages may be 10–32 lines); 300/1200 baud support; and clock. Survey form can be used for ordering or interlibrary loans. Autodelete removes old messages (110 messages may be active on system at one time). Remote operation and maintenance are built-in capabilities, and special chip plugs into Apple I/O port, making unauthorized copying (by people who did not purchase the program) impossible.

A networking system, *ACCESS* transfers up to 100 messages or forms between systems automatically, at any specified time of day or night. (Only text files may be sent, however, since system does not support other types of file transfers, such as programs.) System does not support a hard disk, but add-on module will support a third Apple drive. Another apparent limitation is 12 text files (with add-on file module).

System is easier to handle than PMS, especially since it requries less programming.

Documentation: Manual explains all features of system and start-up.

Related programs: Auxiliary file program, using three drives, enables user to create text files online.

Name: **ASCII Express**

Program type: Online utility

Vendor: United Software Industries

Cost: $129.95, Apple DOS 3.3, ProDOS or Pascal
$149.95, Apple CP/M
$84.95, IBM PC MS DOS

Hardware
requirements: Apple II series; IBM PC; Hayes micromodem II or Smartmodem

Capacity: 300/1200/2400 baud

Description: This excellent online utility performs many important functions when connected to another computer system: uploading, downloading, "macros" (automatic typing), buffer storage, error checking, block send mode, password protection, offline editing, and built-in line editing. System comes with large number of defaults for extensive customization, and supports a Hayes Smartmodem. System may be set up as electronic mail node (unattended), under password control.

ASCII is easy to learn, though its many option screens and use of macros require patience. Large buffer automatically saves text to disk when filled.

Documentation: Extensive directory (but no index) and large table of contents.

Name: **BBS-PC**

Program type: Bulletin board system

Vendor: Micro-Systems Software, Inc.

Cost: $249

Hardware
requirements: IBM PC, XT, PCjr., and compatibles, 256K

Description: System supports electronic mail, program and data file exchanges, 16 subboards (message divisions), four file transfer protocols for uploading and downloading to board, and a second modem (used by system to dial out, even if someone has dialed in). Levels (areas) of access are 256, as assigned by system operator, which makes it easy to exclude write privileges to all but selected callers. Big advantage is that system operator can review material before it's put in public area. Many BBS features are also available, including autodeletion of old messages.

Documentation: Manual of operating instructions describes features and procedures.

Name: **EasyNet**

Program type: Online public access telecommunications

Vendor: EasyNet

Cost: $550, annual subscription fee (includes $100 in searches)
$5 usage fee per successful search
20¢ per minute Telenet connect fee

Hardware requirements: Any microcomputer with modem

Description: This online search utility is intended for public access. No software is used at local site; instead, users dial database service, log on with credit card, and are connected with selected database (any of 700). Libraries receive 5 percent credit on searches. Annual fee includes 25 user guides.

Flustered users may type in "SOS" for help from operator (online). System provides users access to online databases without involving librarian. Each search returns 10 most current references. User may let *EasyNet* pick database, or user may pick database, even during walkthrough (which helps complete search). One reference may be full text, or (for extra fee) as many texts as desired. Recently, system allows searching by field instead of through entire database. This option is also menu driven.

Name: **GBBS** (Great Bulletin Board System)

Program type: Bulletin board system

Vendor: Micro Data Products

Cost: $99.95, Apple version
$49.95, advanced file transfer system module
$49.95, text adventure game system module
$95.00, GBBS PC (MS-DOS 2.0 and higher), 256K RAM

Hardware requirements: Apple II series with clock card; DOS and ProDOS versions available; IBM PC with 256K, MS-DOS

Used at: Maywood Public Library
121 S. Fifth Ave.
Maywood, IL 60153
312-343-1847
Contact: Patrick R. Dewey

Description: This menu-driven program may be customized without difficulty by following the directions and making the proper selections. Options include an unlimited number of multiple boards, automatic kill of messages, online surveys, Xmodem and ASCII download protocols, obscenity filter, and automatic assignment of passwords. The multiple board option is being used on Lincolnet, a BBS of the Suburban Library System (operated at the Maywood Public Library). A separate board is available for librarians, the public, children's services, etc. Other boards will be added as required. The system supports 300/1200 baud modems.

Documentation: Looseleaf notebook contains start-up instructions and suggestions for customizing the program code.

Name: **MICROsearch**

Program type: Database (local ERIC search system)

Vendor: ERIC Clearinghouse on Information Resources

Cost: Consult vendor

Hardware requirements: Apple II series, 48K; one disk drive. Printer useful, but optional

Description: This database system permits in-house searching of segments of ERIC database on data diskettes, by author, key title words, and descriptors from ERIC *Thesaurus*. Three logical operators may be used: AND, OR, and NOT; and right-hand truncation. Once search terms have been entered, they may be saved and used again, as other data diskettes are used. Each disk contains 200 to 300 bibliographic records from *Resources in Education* and *Current Index to Journals in Education.* Each contains accession number, author, title, journal citation, descriptors, and identifiers. Regrettably, no abstracts are available because of inadequate disk space (according to publisher). A wonderful tool for students and patrons.

Documentation: Thirty-four–page manual

Name: **PC/Net LINK**

Program type: Online utility

Vendor: Informatics General Corp.

Cost: $500, with Telios
$400, *PC/Net* only
$30, manual only

Hardware requirements: IBM PC, 128K; M300; 10MB hard disk; 1200 baud Smartmodem (or Hayes-compatible equipment); printer

Description: This package has many excellent features, including upload/download, online index of search suggestions, automatic dialing, and creation and storage of search strategies.

Documentation: Excellent looseleaf binder contains user guide and administration manual.

Name: **People's Message System**

Program type: Electronic bulletin board system

Vendor: Bill Blue, Marilla Corp.

Cost: $300

Hardware requirements: Apple II+, IIe, 64K; CCS or Mountain Hardware clock; two disk drives; Hayes 300 baud modem. Will work with hard drive; requires three floppy drives (or hard drive) for uploading module.

Used at: North-Pulaski Branch Library
4041 W. North
Chicago, IL 60639
312-235-2727

Maywood Public Library
121 S. Fifth Ave.
Maywood, IL 60153
312-343-1847

Description: Program has been in continuous use since 1981 at North-Pulaski branch of Chicago Public Library, and some accounts of its operation are listed below. Generally a good program, though electronic bulletin board system (the purpose of this program) should not be started by novices. Usually, those who operate this system should know elementary (Applesoft), basic programming.

System allows for message base, posting of bulletins and articles, and uploading/downloading of text. Also maintains log file of callers, comment file, and has impressive array of other features, including excellent error-trapping device (lack of which is a common failing of such programs). Inordinate tinkering will always be associated with any BBS operation, and PMS is no exception. It supports a fixed disk, if one is available, but will not support 1200 baud. Vendor support is marginal at best. Text for messages is in form of ASCII files, and so any good word processor can be used for maintaining data files. Online public access database can be a good investment for public relations. The PMS is fairly resistant to "crashers" and "hackers."

Documentation: Material which accompanies program discusses many features and important considerations for running the program; unfortunately, it was not written for the novice. It presumes a high level of proficiency with such programs.

Related
programs: Best source of information about the many BBS programs is *Bulletin Board Systems,* a newsletter published by Meckler (which has annual listing).

Additional
information: Dewey, Patrick. "The Electronic Bulletin Board Arrives at the Public Library," *Library High Tech,* Spring 1984, p. 13.

Name: **Pro-Search**

Program type: Online utility

Vendor:	Personal Bibliographic Software, Inc.
Cost:	$495
	$295, if purchased with another PBS program
	$19.95, sample disk

Hardware
requirements: IBM PC with two double-side disk drives; IBM PC, XT, AT, with one double-side disk drive and one fixed drive, or compatible; minimum RAM 256K, DOS 2.0 or later; Hayes Smartmodem 300, 1200, 1200B, or 2400, or any acoustic modem

Description: This program has many features, including autolog for up to 20 systems, online help with Dialog and BRS, data buffer, upload, download, ability to create offline search, print records online or offline, and much more. Configuration is quick and simple, and formulating search strategy offline can save money and time. Strategies may be saved to disk or printed out. Perhaps major benefit is the online catalog. Users may automate selection of database they wish to access. Each database is represented on electronic card which contains abstract of online charges, nature of database, etc.

By simple keystroke, *Pro-Search* dials up and connects with database. Because abstracts and database information go out of date quickly, diskette updates may be purchased as a package (6 updates per year) or per set, whenever desired. Data disks cover biology and medicine, arts, education and social sciences, business, government and news, and engineering, mathematics, and physical sciences. Utilities disk is separate. Data saved with the buffer may be coded for later use with a word processor or other application.

Documentation: Notebook details system's capabilities and explains configuration and advanced utilities.

Additional
information: *"Pro-Search* Simplifies DIALOG and BRS Searching," *American Libraries,* December 1985, p. 825.

Name:	**Search Helper**
Program type:	Online utility

Vendor: Information Access Company

Cost: $1950 (700 searches), $1250 (300 searches); includes software. Free demonstration package simulates online connection.

Hardware requirements: Apple II series; IBM PC, XT; Eagle. Bizcomp 1012 external modem, 1200 baud Smartmodem, or Hayes compatible modems

Description: This easy-to-use package provides public access to seven databases: Magazine Index, National Newspaper Index, Legal Resource Index, Trade & Industry Index, Management Contents, Computer Database, and Newsearch. Impressive system; does all dialing and log-on procedures. Users may even use Boolean operators as they enter selections offline: choosing database (among the 7 listed above), selecting "person" or "subject," then specifying particular "person" or "subject," including additional search criteria if desired. Program does the rest and prints the results. Typically, patrons receive 20 most recent citations in a few minutes, at a fixed cost (see above).

Additional information: Bailey, Bill. "Search Helper" (review), *Apple Library Users Group Newsletter,* April 1985, p. 27.

Tenopir, Carol. "IAC's Document Delivery and More," *Library Journal,* June 1, 1984, p. 1104.

Name: **Smartcom I/II**

Program type: Communications

Vendor: Hayes Microcomputer Products, Inc.

Cost: $149, Macintosh. Other versions come bundled with modem.

Hardware requirements: Apple II series; IBM PC; Macintosh (360K); Smartcom I: Hayes Micromodem IIe (300 baud), Smartcom II: Hayes Smartmodem (300/1200 baud)

Description: *Smartcom I,* though a less sophisticated version of *Smartcom II,* has enough power for most users. Features include support of DOS 3.3, Pascal, CP/M 2.2 and ALS CP/M 2.2 operating systems, answering and originating calls, simple file creation, parameter management, printer on/off, and much more. Unfortunately, stores only three telephone numbers for autodial. If used with Micromodem IIe, *Smartcom I* will provide Touch Tone dialing and speaker output.

Smartcom II, an impressive package, will originate and answer calls; create, list, receive, or send a file; turn printer on and off; change parameters. Program, menu driven and easy to operate, prints exactly what is on the screen at any time. Big advantage of *Smartcom II* is the ease with which it can be set up and ability to store several dozen telephone numbers, with full complement of parameters for each, making one-finger operation very nearly a reality.

Macintosh version provides the same excellent utilities, through convenience of the Mac Mouse. Icons (symbols) across the bottom of screen let one choose printer control, editing, dialing, disk functions, etc. Will support 300, 1200, or 2400 baud.

Documentation: Excellent tab-indexed manual, with complete installation and operation instructions.

Database Management

Introduction

For our purposes, a database is an organized group of data or facts—not unfamiliar to librarians in many other forms (usually as a reference book or file cabinet), but increasingly as automated circulation systems and microcomputer-based information and referral systems, and of course as online files accessed by telecommunications. The software which organizes and recalls the data is the *database program,* and the facts themselves comprise the *database.* The "hierarchy" of a database is the *file* as a whole, *records* (groups of facts associated with one entry, such as the name, address, phone number, etc., of one person), and *field* (each datum or part of a record).

Another way to visualize a database is to look at it as a 3 × 5 card file. The box of cards is the database, each card is a record, and each item on each card is a field.

Creating an electronic database consists of storing, updating, and finding (retrieving) the data once they are stored. Different systems do this in different ways and with different degrees of success, which is another way of saying that some database systems are more sophisticated than others. Major differences arise in the time required to sort the file, record capacity, field length and number, search capability, indexing, flexibility in data entry, and formatting or making reports (both to screen and to paper).

In a recent survey, I found that librarians were using microcomputer database systems (of one type or another) for

Information and referral (essentially an automated card file)	Mailing lists
	Newspaper indexing
	Personnel lists
Inventory	Periodical lists
Book orders	Phone lists
Career catalogs	Phone survey

Friends-of-libraries files   Union lists of large-print
Summer-reading participants   books for a group of libraries
Local organizations   Videotape catalogs
Community file lists   Wall charts for public reference

The essential aspects of the creation and maintenance of a database are collecting data, designing the database, inputting the data, editing the database, and revising and updating the data as needed. Obviously, at some point before the database is created, it is necessary to purchase a software package. How can you know which type to buy—or whether the package you finally select is the best one to do the job? A good approach is to think in terms of levels of software, and then to choose a package in a level needed to do the job.

Levels of Database Management Systems

Specialized database systems now exist for just about any function: cataloging, accessions, overdues, mailing lists, etc. With such a system (which usually is inexpensive), the disk is popped into the drive and data entry begins. Some of these systems offer flexibility in data entry and printout format. Record capacity varies. Unfortunately, nearly all are single-function programs (like arcade machines) and will refuse to do anything but their single-minded task. The *Vanlove* directory for IBM software lists 148 specialized systems, and the Apple directory lists 50. The IBM directory has 48 systems under the single category "Mailing List"!

File management programs, which allow the user greater flexibility, come in various "strengths," but all have one thing in common: they can customize your database, to some extent. That is, you can usually decide on the number of fields and lengths, as well as name them. It is usually possible to customize the printout format as well, but that varies greatly, according to the program. Control over page margins, column widths, etc., is usually characteristic of file management programs. Therefore, single programs can have multiple uses: name and address lists, catalog card files, inventory lists, etc.

Relational database management systems are sometimes referred to by purists as the only true or real database management systems. By this they mean that these systems have the ability to access more than one file at a time (up to 4 in *dBase II* and up to 12 in *dBase III*). Information in several files can thereby be brought together for analysis, if the two files have a common field or code (such as a customer number). Clearly, these are the most sophisticated and powerful database systems, and are used for the most advanced projects. They are also the most difficult to master, sometimes requiring weeks or longer to understand the fundamentals of the programming language, which is necessary to get the system to do what you want (or do anything at all, for that matter). Sometimes, it is possible to purchase "templates" (programs) directly from publishers to do what is required, without any programming (see "Miscellaneous" chapter of this volume for sources of some templates).

It is important to remember (as if we could forget!) that library needs are not the needs of the world in general, and, as a result, special database systems, both specialized and flexible, have been developed specifically for information centers. Of special interest is *CAIRS* and *Inmagic* (listed below).

Sources of Additional Information

"Data Management Software," *Library Technology Reports,* September–October 1983, p. 453.

Ensor, Pat. "The Expanding Use of Computers in Reference Service," *RQ,* Summer 1982, p. 365.

Faulkner, Ronnie W. "dBase III and Newspaper Indexing," *Library Software Review,* 4, no. 5:280.

Fox, Kathleen. "Database-Management Software for Apple II Systems," *Library Software Review,* 3, no. 3:346.

Gillespie, Jim. "Fine Tuning the Book Budget with *dBase* and *SuperCalc*," *Small Computers in Libraries,* May 1985, p. 6.

Lundeen, Gerald, and Carol Tenopir. "Microcomputer Software for In-House Databases: Four Top Packages," *Online,* September 1985, p. 30.

Shroder, Emelie J. "Community Information in the '80s: Towards Automation of Information and Referral Files," *RQ,* Winter 1981, p. 135.

The Ratings Book: IBM PC Database and File Management Programs, 1984/85 ed., Software Digest, 1984.

Tenopir, Carol. "Identification and Evaluation of Software for Microcomputer-Based In-House Databases," *Information Technology and Libraries,* March 1984, p. 21.

Tenopir, Carol, "In-House Databases II: Evaluating and Choosing Software," *Library Journal,* May 1, 1983, p. 885.

Reviews

Art Prints Inventory

AV Equipment Inventory

Authex

Bookends

CAIRS

DB Master (3 Systems)

dBase II and III

Fiction Finder

The Index

InfoQuest OPAC

InMagic/Biblio

List Handler

Name:	**Art Prints Inventory**
Program type:	Media inventory
Vendor:	Media Center Factory
Cost:	$29.95
Hardware requirements:	Apple II series; IBM PC; TRS-80 Model 3 or 4
Capacity:	1150 records with two drives, 900 with one drive (800 on the TRS 80)
Description:	Functions of this specialized, menu-driven database for maintaining record of art prints include a record of the artist's last name (15 characters), artist's first name (15), call number (10), title (30), folder number (10), print number (10), and subject (20). Sort and search permitted by every field, except artist's first name; string searching (partial entry) or searching by record number is also permitted. *Art Prints Inventory* is extremely simple and easy-to-use database, performing single function for this special need.
Documentation:	Twelve-page pamphlet

Name:	**AV Equipment Inventory**
Program type:	Inventory
Vendor:	Media Center Factory

Cost: $29.95

Hardware
requirements: Apple II series; IBM PC; TRS-80 Model 3 or 4

Capacity: 1150 records with two drives, 900 with one drive (800 on TRS-80)

Description: This specialized, menu-driven database maintains a record of audiovisual equipment and uses the following data fields: type of equipment (20 characters), brand (15), model (10), serial number (12), jobber/vendor (12), cost (8), date received (8), source of funds (10), room locations (15). Program is easy to operate. Users may add or delete items, sort and print, query (i.e., search for item by its unique number), or search by field (e.g., if all equipment of a certain type or in one room). Because program is memory- or RAM-based file, it is fairly fast.

Documentation: Twelve-page pamphlet

Name: **Authex**

Program type: Indexing system

Vendor: Reference Press

Cost: $75. Demonstration disk, $25

Hardware
requirements: IBM PC, 128K, plus two 320K floppies or one floppy with 10/20 MB hard disk, printer

Used at: Special Collections Department
Strozier Library
Drawer A
University of Florida
Belle Grade, FL 33430
305-996-3061

Capacity: 32,000 records, 16 fields, 2500 characters per field

Description: Primary function of this menu-driven, relatively user-friendly program is indexing periodicals. According to its manual, program is "used effectively to prepare vertical file indexes, current awareness reports, newspaper indexes, special collections catalogues, and bibliographies." As part of *Authex* system, it employs online authority file which accommodates subjects and names and associated cross-references. This means that each heading is stored only once in the database. System also provides multiple-level subheadings, and adds cross-references automatically. Some obvious uses include indexing of topical magazines for the public or newspapers for history collections for general/local information.

See and *See also* references by *Authex* does not permit "blind" references, and its job of indexing, once data have been entered, may take several hours (or more). Index formats are full subject or title, author, subject/series title, publisher, titles for proofreading, subject index for proofreading, corporate author, English-language titles, French-language author, access number, and a spare. To help in editing once data have been entered, *Authex* will print out draft for proofreading.

Possible drawback is lack of online search. Online tutorials briefly explain major functions.

Documentation:	Excellent 100-page manual gives full details on use and operation of *Authex,* including utilities, examples of printouts, etc.
Related programs:	Add-on modules of subject headings, including *Canadian Subject Headings* ($30), *Vertical File Subject Headings* ($30), *Museum and Archive Subject Authority* ($35), *Scientific and Technical Subject Headings* ($35), and *Juvenile Subject Headings* ($30). Program to enable *Authex* online use with elementary logic is being developed. Vendor says this module will cost approximately $50.

Name:	**Bookends**
Program type:	Card file
Vendor:	Sensible Software, Inc.

Cost: $124.95

Hardware
requirements: Apple II series, 64K, ProDOS (DOS 3.3 version
available upon request); one disk drive

Capacity: 720 characters per field (except classification)
255 records per file (but several files may be chained
together to form longer file)

Description: Specialized, easy-to-use system, coupled with standard
record format, *Bookends* is a RAM database (i.e., entire
file is in memory at one time). Necessary to access disk
only when saving or loading a file — which works for and
against program: operations such as searching a file are
swift, but limits on number of records in a file are
severe. This menu-driven program will serve the librarian who wants simple, easy system for maintaining small
file of book and periodical references which can be
easily updated (basically, information and referral).

Bookends has two predetermined limits — maximum 255 references per file or whatever may be in
memory — which tend to build many small files (though
it is possible to chain most functions together, enabling
automatic search from one file to next). Fields (author,
title, journal, volume, page number, date, publisher,
keywords, location, abstract) may be altered as required. Once data have been entered, word processing
capability can make corrections in text, rather than completely redo entry or field (delete to end of line, delete
one character, cursor control, insert line, move to beginning or end of file).

Bookends has good retrieval capability and flexibility, and is generally well done. Searching is by
author field, keyword field, or universal (all fields).

Documentation: Looseleaf notebook has extensive instructions on how to
use *Bookends,* including tutorial.

Name: **Computer Assisted Information/Library Retrieval
Systems (Micro-CAIRS)**

Program type: Database management system

Vendor: Information/Documentation, Inc.

Cost: Consult vendor. Prices start at $1400, and may include microcomputer (if desired).

Hardware requirements: IBM PC, XT, compatibles, with minimum 5MB, 256K RAM, but will work on many systems. Manufacturer will "bundle" hardware and software as single unit, so you need deal with only one vendor.

Used at: Suburban Library System
125 Tower Dr.
Burr Ridge, IL 60521
Contact Sally Webb
312-325-6640

Capacity: Unlimited (only real limit is disk space)

Description: Spectacular database management system available to libraries, it is adapted from program *(CAIRS)* used originally on mainframe computers and comes configured from manufacturer. Powerful, allows wide range of options, is easy to use, flexible, and may be accessed online or as remote system as single- or multi-user system. Has built-in word processor, fast search capability, online help files, and is user friendly. Excellent online database, requires no programming.

One application is at Suburban Library System, where it maintains large database of Illinois libraries and allows retrieval of many types of data about libraries. However, it is suitable for special libraries and has many uses: word processing, report generation, acquisitions, claims, catalog, reference, circulation, etc. Indexing may be fully automatic or relational, and built-in thesaurus helps this function. Has its own security system.

Documentation: System comes completely configured and user can begin entry immediately. Yearly service contract guarantees support from vendor, though documentation gives adequate directions for most procedures.

Name: **DB Master 4 Plus; Advanced DB Master; DB Master Macintosh**

Program type: Database management system

Vendor: Stoneware, Inc.

Cost: $350, *DB Master 4 Plus*
$595, *Advanced DB Master* (IBM PC)
$195, *DB Master Macintosh*

Hardware
requirements: Plus Apple II+, IIe, IIc, 64K *(DB Master 4 Plus)*; IBM
PC, 256K *(Advanced DB Master);* Macintosh *(DB
Master Macintosh)*

Capacity: See below

Used at: Bozeman Public Library
220 E. Lamme
Bozeman, MT 59715
406-586-4787

Description: *DB Master* is good choice as relational database system
(for explanation of this term, see introduction to this
chapter) because of its peripheral programs, especially
many templates created and used by libraries (reviewed
elsewhere in this volume). Difficult in this space to ex-
pound properly upon three hardware versions, so Apple
II version will be discussed and other two packages sum-
marized according to major differences.

DB Master, a multidisk database system, can
handle more than one disk—up to 100 in Apple version—and it files data by "indexed sequential access
method," in which user defines a "screen" or form,
which is thereafter simply filled in during data entry.
Capacity with regular *DB Master 4 Plus* is 100 fields and
1020 bytes per record, up to 9 user-defined screen pages
per record, and up to 6-field sort at one time. However,
system is very difficult to learn, requiring involved
understanding of accompanying tutorial.

Macintosh version has mouse, different fonts, and
pull-down windows to make use easy and convenient.
Forms are still designed, along with report formats.
Data are compatible with *MacWrite* and other Macintosh
programs. Supports up to 44 disks of 400K each, or 20
megabytes, on a hard disk. Record may be up to 3000
characters, 100 fields, or 100 screen lines. Twenty
selection criteria may be used for search. Maximum
report width is 255 characters; 100 fields per record.

Advanced DB Master, an IBM PC program, handles up to 16 megabytes of data; records may be 3000 characters and up to 250 fields.

It is difficult to manage database that is spread across dozens of diskettes, and so hard disk may be essential.

Documentation: Start-up, reference, and feature material for each version

Related
programs: *DB Master Templates,* for libraries (see "Miscellaneous" chapter of this volume.)

Additional
information: "Using a Microcomputer to Control a Paperback Collection," *Apple Library Users Group,* October 1985, p. 52.

Name: **dBase II**

Program type: Database management system

Vendor: Ashton-Tate

Cost: $495 (but often discounted to $350 or less)

Hardware
requirements: Apple II series (with CP/M), IBM PC

Used at: University of Arizona (*Small Computers in Libraries,* May 1983) for indexing newspaper

Capacity: 65,000 records
32 fields per record
1000 characters per record

Description: With *dBase II,* a multipurpose system, users may open two files at one time (up to 65,000 records in each). Single records may be 1000 characters, which for most libraries is more than sufficient for accounting, indexing, list management, or other uses. Some libraries use *dBase II* to create whole circulation systems (some application programs are written in *dBase,* giving it less status as database management than as computer language). Can be used two ways: as list or file handler to "create" file of records, which may then be indexed, sorted, and manipulated, or programming language, which permits groups of commands (essentially macros) to be stored as command file, then executed like any other program. This makes it possible to create almost any sort of library program, including acquisitions, cataloging, budgeting, and circulation.

Relational component (see introduction to this chapter for explanation of this term) of *dBase* makes it possible to draw data from more than one file, provided two files are linked by common field. If a library has two files of customers for two functions (e.g., reserve and overdue lists), but each has a common field (say, the patron's library card number), it is always possible to pull data from both files, simultaneously, for same customer.

It is true that *dBase* can handle all applications mentioned above, but must be kept in mind that a computer and a database program will not do anything on their own; other resources must be applied, and the first resource is time to learn the system. *dBase* requires struggle, for considerable time, before one comes to terms with it. If the correct templates or command files can be found, much of this difficulty may be bypassed. In recent years, Ashton-Tate has added online help screens and improved the documentation (see *dBase III*, below), but users must learn and deal with a programming language and bulky documentation. Such programs as *dBase,* or other advanced systems, have many uses, and investment in time and energy will repay itself over many years of use. (People who want to use a database manager more quickly should look to less complicated systems.) *dBase II* includes demonstration package which may be previewed before plastic package is unwrapped.

Documentation: Apple version of *dBase II* comes with about 200 pages of documentation, online tutorial, and command card for quick reference.

Related
programs: Hundreds of templates or specialized *dBase* programs may be ordered separately from many vendors. Ashton-Tate offers program, *dBase/Answer,* which permits

dBase II to be used online. Since many people use *dBase,* there are user groups, vendors, and others to turn to for help.

Templates: Ashton-Tate supplies list of templates for *dBase II* which are manufactured by other companies: *Application Junction: A Catalog of RunTime Applications.* (Many such programs, however, cost more than *dBase* itself.) With such templates and programs, it is possible to take advantage of the power of *dBase* and the ease of using off-the-shelf programs.

Additional
information: Baker, Richard H. *How to Run Your Business with* dBase. TAB, 1984.

Chen, Ching-chih, and Barbara DeYoung. dBase *Workbook for Libraries.* MicroUse Information, 1984.

Stultz, Russell A. *The Illustrated* dBase II *Book.* Prentice-Hall, 1984.

Name: **dBase III**

Program type: Database management system

Vendor: Ashton-Tate

Cost: $795

Hardware
requirements: IBM PC XT (256K RAM minimum) or any PC DOS (2.0 or up) or MS DOS computer (Compaq, Columbia, Corona, Eagle PC). Also requires two 360K floppy disk drives or one 360K disk drive, hard disk drive, and 80-column printer. (Ashton-Tate is trying to eliminate necessity to boot from master floppy disk in hard disk systems.)

Used at: Central Piedmont Community College Library
Box 35009
Charlotte, NC 28235
Contact: Phoebe Oplinger, Library Director
704-373-6883

Capacity: 1 billion records
4000 characters per record

128 fields per record

4 files opened at one time

Description: *dBase III* is in some ways the ultimate management system, beyond the limits of *dBase II* and most other systems. Speed (sort time), records allowed, and number of files which may be opened simultaneously, etc., have all been increased or improved, and *dBase III* is totally menu driven. However attractive, it is difficult to learn and operate, and comes with massive documentation. Operates only on IBM PC XT (or compatibles). Comes with two copies of system master and one disk of sample programs and utilities. Like many other expensive programs, *dBase III* is "shrink-wrapped": by breaking the seal on package, you accept the terms of the transaction, and the software may not be returned.

Documentation: 500-page manual is thorough and eventually gets users to point where they can enter and store data, create their own programs, and perform database "miracles." Tutorial is 217 pages. Reference section has detailed listing and explanation of each major *dBase* command, glossary, and index. Separate booklet guides users through conversion from *dBase II* to *dBase III* files. Standup steno pad comes as "Quick Reference Chart."

Additional
information: Clifford, Michael J. *Managing with* dBase III. Sams, 1985.

Faulkner, Ronnie W. *"dBase III* and Newspaper Indexing," *Library Software Review,* September/October 1985, p. 280.

Jones, Edward. *Using* dBase III. McGraw-Hill, 1985.

Simpson, Alan. *Advanced Techniques in* dBase III. Sybex, 1985.

Weber Systems Staff. dBase III *User's Handbook.* Ballantine, 1985.

Name: **Fiction Finder**

Program type: Database management

Vendor: Calico

Cost: $39.95

Hardware
requirements: Apple II series

Description: Produces customized lists of reading materials for patrons or teachers—up to 1000 book titles coded by 27 categories (westerns, romances, etc.), and each category may be classified 8 ways (e.g., college level, long, short, easy reading, etc.). Materials selected by program may be printed out or viewed on screen.

Documentation: Small booklet explains all.

Name: **The Index**

Program type: Database management system
Online card catalog system

Vendor: Media Center Factory

Cost: $69.95

Hardware
requirements: Apple II series; Commodore 64; IBM PC; TRS-80 Model 3 or 4.

Capacity: 1150 records with two drives, 800 records with one drive

Description: Perhaps smallest card catalog system around, is used primarily in media center or very small library. Maintains inventory of books and other materials, with space for author (25 characters), title (35), main and secondary subjects fields (20 characters each), and call number (10). Menu-driven operation includes data entry or deletion, and search or sort functions by any field. Corrections or deletions must be made by record number; changes, however, may be made by field—not entire entry. Finding record number is easy if printout has been made, or database may be scrolled on screen. *The Index* uses *Diversi-DOS,* a high-speed operating system registered for use with this program.

Documentation: Eleven-page pamphlet

Name:	**InfoQUEST OPAC** (Online Public Access Catalog)
Program type:	Online public access catalog
Vendor:	Utlas, Inc.
Cost:	Consult vendor.

Hardware
requirements: IBM PC, 256K; PCDOS 2.1; one floppy disk drive minimum, Tallgrass hard disk drive with tape drive unit (1 megabyte per 1000 titles recommended); Epson FX80 or RX80 printer (printer not required)

Capacity: 25,000 records

Description: This unusual program is only for users of Utlas *Catalogue Support System,* and provides library with local online public access catalog in steps. Step 1 is creation of database (in full MARC format) on Utlas central system. Database is then matched against LC name and subject authority files (step 2), and downloaded (step 3) to IBM PC via tape cartridge or diskette, and then is available locally. Uses Ocelot Database Management System (Ocelot Computer Systems) and conforms to CODASYL network database standard.

Even though library's equipment and technology may change or become obsolete, database, maintained on Utlas computer, can be modified to meet needs. Supports catalog use statistics (number and type of searches, which cumulate until computer is reset). System is menu driven, and search (by patron) may be conducted by author, subject, or title. Numeric fields may also be searched—LCCN, call number, ISBN, and RSN (unique Record Sequence Number assigned to a record by CATSS system)—but only by staff with the password. Screen prompts provide easy-to-understand language, including online help menus. Many parts of display may be modified to meet with local approval, including entire help menu, and some display messages may be modified. After a search entry, number of hits is displayed and users have option to view records in brief, full, or extended full mode, and to scroll forward or back. Can also produce *See* and *See also* references with Utlas authority control system.

Additional
information: Campbell, Bonnie. *"InfoQUEST*: An Online Catalog for
Small Libraries," *Library Hi Tech,* issue 7, 1984, p. 41.

Powell, Wyley, and Norville Webb. "UTLAS—A High
Tech Success Story," *Technicalities,* October 1984,
p. 1.

Name: **InMagic/Biblio**

Program type: Database management

Vendor: InMagic, Inc.

Cost: *InMagic:* $975
Biblio: $145 (special library database models)
TestMagic: $65 (demonstrator with documentation)

Hardware
requirements: IBM PC, XT, AT (MSDOS, PODOS 2.0 up), and compatibles; Wang PC; DEC Rainbow; 256K required on
all machines

Used at: Savage Information Services
608 Silver Spur Rd.
Suite 310
Rolling Hills Estates, CA 90274
213-377-5032

Capacity: Limited only by the disk drive in use

Description: *InMagic* allows text records of variable length, fields
may be any length, and reports may be custom for-
matted. Though designed for special libraries, can perform many functions in public, academic, or school
libraries. *InMagic* allows Boolean operators for searching, keyword or term indexing on any field, unlimited
number of records in database, online help screens and
tutorials, and flexible report generator for custom
presentations. "User Service" contract can be purchased
for 10 percent annually, and includes program updates.

Biblio, a library-specific package, will produce
online catalog, orders database, serial control, and circulation data. *Orders* (acquisitions module), a full-
service system, provides full tracking, beginning with
purchase request, monitoring receipt of order, tracking

budget expenditure, sending status requests and claims to vendors, and status reports. Activity and backup reports may be generated. At appropriate time, cataloging information may be sent to main database, *Catlog*. System provides for printing bibliographies, book and spine labels, shelflist cards, and inventory control printouts.

Serial, besides producing routing slips, holdings lists, and title and subject bibliographies, maintains file of subscription costs and names to which they are charged (and much more). *Circ*, a circulation control and management model, tracks items lent to persons from a corporation library. *Catlog*, an online catalog management system, provides unlimited number of subject headings, location codes, classification numbers, contract numbers, and spine label information.

Documentation: *InMagic* comes with excellent manual of several hundred pages, well organized, clearly written, and indexed; includes glossary, data structure documentation worksheet, and installation procedures.

Additional
information: Lundeen, Gerald, and Carol Tenopir. "Microcomputer-Based Library Catalog Software," *Microcomputers for Information Management*, September 1984, p. 215.

Name: **List Handler**

Program type: Database management system

Vendor: Silicon Valley Systems, Inc.

Cost: $49.95

Hardware
requirements: Apple II series. Program uses softvideo driver for producing 70 columns on 40-column screen, allows for a printer in any of several slots, and up to 8 disk drives.

Used at: Marin County (Calif.) Free Library
415-499-6056

Richland County (Wis.) Public Library
(for standing orders)
803-799-9084

Capacity: 3000 records per disk (address file), 255 fields or 4000 characters per record (field may be up to 200 characters)

Description: Extremely easy-to-use program has much more power than price suggests. Will automate production of mailing lists and form letters, as well as print lists. Will also maintain materials-on-order (acquisitions) file (see reference below). Tutorial disk included. Problems with this program include inability to sort two fields at once, lack of statistical reports, inability to monitor how much disk space remains. However, data may be expanded to more than one disk, so it is not necessary to "push disk to limit."

Documentation: Seventy-three–page manual with examples and complete instructions

Additional
information: Allman, Linda, and Gretchen L. Freeman. "Standing Orders with *Listhandler," Small Computers in Libraries,* October 1984, p. 8. Readers are urged to consult this excellent article before purchasing *List Handler*.

Integrated Software

Introduction

In the beginning there were individual software packages: spreadsheets, word processors, database managers, and others. Each did its particular thing—sometimes well, sometimes not—but almost always alone. In 1982 that all changed, with the advent of *Context MBA,* which had "integrated software." The understanding of this term has become confused; it now means a group of software packages that "work together in some way." As it turned out, *MBA* worked better than many of the so-called integrated packages that have come along since. Integration is a wholly new area (try to find "integrated software" in a computer dictionary). Manufacturers of integrated software have no standard definition, so different packages do different things, and some of them do the same things, but differently.

Some of the ways in which software is integrated are commonality of commands, exchange or sharing of data, product families, and operating environments (also known as "integrators"), which is to say "some software is more integrated than others." There are also features which look like integration but aren't, such as "concurrent" software and "bundled" software.

Some systems have the obvious advantage that we need not learn two or three sets of commands to do two or three different things. With some systems, there is no need to illustrate a report with a pie or bar chart, to cut and paste data from a spread sheet, since they may be inserted automatically into the report, generated by the word processor module. If a communications module is used, data may be "zapped" through the telephone lines without leaving the program. Some software has apparently been "bundled," which is to say that several packages were simply squeezed together and labeled "integrated." There is no guarantee that they will work together properly.

Some packages do not have a word processor, telecommunications, or graphics, and others have spreadsheets and database managers that are inferior to standalone packages. Some integrated software, especially the integrators (discussed below), require so much overhead that they operate more slowly than is tolerable.

One very new and exciting class of software is known as "desktop." These programs generally perform many functions that are associated with desktop work, such as math, note taking, and scheduling. Some even perform integration features by allowing the flow of data from one program into another. Perhaps the most popular of these programs is *SideKick.* Such programs are resident in memory and are visible only when summoned by the operator from within (without exiting) other programs.

Integrators

Another and special set of programs is available, called "integrators," or "do-it-yourself integrated software." With it, we can combine any favorite set of software packages into a cohesive unit. The major advantage of such a system is that it is possible to use programs already owned, and not be forced to switch to new, predetermined programs. One such integrator is *DESQ* (pronounced "desk"), for computers which use a PC DOS (MS DOS) operating system. It works with virtually any IBM software, up to a total of nine programs. Users may even arrange their own menus and command structure. To run a program, it is necessary that *DESQ* have essential information, which it terms "agent." (A number of these programs come predefined, so that many can be up and running with little input from the user: *WordStar, VisiCalc,* etc.) *DESQ* also supports a mouse, if desired. It is also possible to transfer data between applications.

There are also disadvantages to all integrated software, and some of these should be noted. Probably most important is the *probable* need to relearn all major program skills. That can take a lot of time, and pain, especially if a software package has been in use for a long time. Another disadvantage is "settling for less" on some programs. Most of the best packages are not available for the Apple computer, and even fewer for the Apple II+, so that could mean changing computers. And since integrated software is much more complicated than individual packages, it can take much longer to compare and evaluate packages. If you are happy with several standalone packages, there is no real reason to change.

Sources of Additional Information

Gilder, Jules H. *The Integrated Software Book.* Addison-Wesley, 1985.

Reviews

AppleWorks
Framework II
Jazz
LibraryWorks
Lotus 1-2-3/Symphony
PFS Family

Name:	**AppleWorks**
Program type:	Integrated software
Vendor:	Apple Computer, Inc.
Cost:	$250
Hardware requirements:	Apple IIe, IIc, 128K. Also works with special large RAM cards, or II+ with special cards
Used at:	Urban Campus Library Des Moines Area Community College 1100 7th St. Des Moines, IA 50314 515-964-6328
Capacity (database):	750 records of 75 characters each 30 fields per record 1024 characters per record maximum 20 characters per field
(spreadsheet):	999 rows, 127 columns
Description:	*AppleWorks* has three components: word processor, database management, and spreadsheet. Extremely popular among librarians, this program aids learning with three worthwhile packages that must be used one at a time (i.e., no transferring from one package to another without first exiting a current package). Some, however, may wish to purchase a desktop package, such as *Pin-*

point (discussed separately) or *Jeeves*, to enhance basic system.

File must be created for each function, which means there is no direct way to transfer data from, say, the word processor (stripped-down version of *Apple Writer*) to the database manager (a version of *Quick File*). To accomplish this, move a file to the "desktop" (supplied), then move it to another component (there are no pull-down windows). This may not be the best kind of integration (compared to some other systems reviewed in this chapter, it is primitive), but it operates within the range of tolerance for most librarians.

AppleWorks supports ASCII (text) files and DIF (Data Interchange Format), and files from Apple's *Quick File*. Another good feature is standardized structure: it is not necessary to learn separate sets of commands to use modules, though some components have more commands than others (all are easy to use). Although *AppleWorks* does not have graphics or communications capabilities, these may be manually inserted by other programs (listed here). Full-feature word processor requires highlighting blocks before deleting or moving them. Database system is only marginally flexible, allowing (for instance) only 20 characters per field and short record length. Capacity of all these components depends upon RAM storage of the microcomputer.

Documentation: Manual gets you started, though many users may wish to purchase separate book for word processing component (*Apple Writer* is reviewed separately). Overall, *AppleWorks* is excellent value, making integrated access to the three most needed software applications relatively easy. However, database management component will not be sufficient for many. It does not have the power of *dBase* or any other major database manager; nor does *Apple Writer* compare favorably with *Word Perfect* or *WordStar*. For rather standard but good packages for the Apple, quest can stop here.

Related programs: *SpellWorks* (Advanced Logic Systems, $49.95) is spelling and mailmerge program specifically designed for

AppleWorks. Spelling component contains 90,000 words.

Additional
information: Anderson, Eric. *Primer of Library Microcomputing.* Follet Co. Free.

AppleWorks Newsletter. Exclusive Reference, Box 11215, San Diego, Calif. 92110.

Applying AppleWorks. Bristen Press, Box 336, New Hartford, N.Y. 13413. $11.45

Ho, May Lien. *AppleWorks for School Librarians.* Hi Willow Research and Publishing, Box 1801, Fayetteville, Ark. 72702. $20. With diskette of templates (reviewed elsewhere in this volume).

Matthews, Carole Boggs. *AppleWorks Made Easy.* McGraw-Hill, 1985.

Name: **Framework II**

Program type: Integrated software

Vendor: Ashton-Tate

Cost: $695

Hardware
requirements: IBM PC, XT, AT, 384K. Two 360K floppy disk drives, or single floppy drive with fixed disk. Color monitor not required. PC DOS 2.0 or higher.

Capacity: See below

Description: *Framework*, a comprehensive system, contains nearly all major functions associated with a business system: word processing, outlining, spreadsheet, graphics, database management, telecommunications, and macros.

Spreadsheet: 32,000 rows by 32,000 columns, with over 160 built-in commands for full programming and macros.

Database management system allows reading in *dBase II/III* files automatically, filters, faster sorts (200 records in 2 seconds), and much more.

Outlining feature allows for arabic or roman numbering; contains flexible "idea processor," brainstorming tool, and much more.

Graphics may be linked to database or spreadsheet for automatic redrawing when numbers are changed.

Documentation: Hundreds of pages in two manuals. Tutorial has separate tab-indexed sections for each function (mentioned above). Reference manual contains additional sections on printing material, FRED language, procedures, and references to most sections already mentioned, with index and glossary. Five appendixes offer information on installation, list of menus, and more.

Related
programs: *Inside Framework* (Hayden, $49.95) is complete tutorial for use with *Framework*.

Additional
information: Hergert, Douglas. *Mastering Framework*. Sybex, 1985. $21.95.

How to Use Framework (FlipTrack Learning Systems), audiocassette course ($99).

Ashton-Tate offers entire series of self-help books: *Framework: An Introduction, On-the-Job Applications, Programmer's Reference, Introduction to Programming, Developer's Handbook,* and *Framework for Writers.*

Name: **Jazz**

Program type: Integrated software

Vendor: Lotus Development Corporation

Cost: $250

Hardware
requirements: Apple Macintosh

Description: *Jazz* contains word processor, database manager, spreadsheet, business graphics, and communications system, using power and flexibility of Macintosh personal computer (with mouse and windows) to make very impressive system. Since files, windows, fonts, and menus are similar (if not identical) for all modules, system can be learned in short time. Like many other types of integrated software, *Jazz* centers on electronic "desktop" from which an application is selected. Familiar Macintosh icons (symbols) are displayed with their names (e.g., a telephone with "Comm"), but are generally superfluous. Two of the most important features are word processor and database manager (described below).

Word processor: Documents are stored by number, and files are either opened or recalled from disk. Also allows for "boiler plate" (text which is used repeatedly in different documents) and mailmerge. In editing, sections of text are chosen by highlighting them with mouse; then they are removed or copied. Printing is simple: press "Print" on file menu and select parameters (e.g., margins, paper size, etc.). Changing fonts or type size is also simple for advanced word processing features. "HotView," a special feature, allows data to be moved from, say, graphics feature to include graphs, tables, or charts in a report.

Database manager: Data are stored in records and fields format. Because *Jazz* is not a true relational database system, it is best to put all related data in same file, since only one file may be opened at one time. Fields must be defined, with their length. Options (once fields have been defined) are insert field, add field, add record, open cell, field attributes, and field format. Sorting by any field, and ascending or descending order (special sort menu makes this fast and easy). More than one field may be selected for sorting, and each is sorted in turn. *Jazz* database also allows sophisticated sorting of records, by fields defined by certain parameters (e.g., all zip code records above 60601).

Additional information:	Berry, Timothy. *Jazz: The Inside Track.* McGraw-Hill, 1985. $18.95

Name:	**LibraryWorks**
Program type:	Template package
Vendor:	Androm Associates
Cost:	$21.95 (prepay); $24.95 (regular), $1.25 postage and handling

Hardware
requirements: Apple IIe/c, 128K, or II+ with Videx expander program and Legend or Tital add-on RAM board; *AppleWorks*

Description: This set of templates covers wide area—form letters, acquisitions, catalog cards, union lists, statistics, budgeting, reference, technical services, and much more. Most files work with database management component of *AppleWorks*, but there's a spreadsheet (e.g., budgeting components), and form letters work with word processor. Excellent idea and practical for many users, but in many ways an idea or example book rather than book of full-fledged, ready-to-use templates. Some templates can perhaps be used immediately, but some are merely "one-liners" around which you can build your structure. Has various library uses, including bibliography creation, acquisitions, catalog card production, and even small library online catalog.

Documentation: Disk of templates is accompanied by 43-page indexed booklet with step-by-step instructions for the word processor, database manager, and spreadsheet in the *AppleWorks* program. List of add-ons, such as mailmerge, Spelling Checkers, and graphics, is appended.

Name: **Lotus 1-2-3/Symphony**

Program type: Integrated software

Vendor: Lotus Development Corporation

Cost: $250

Hardware
requirements: *Lotus:* IBM PC (192K)
Symphony: IBM PC (320K)

Used at: James Elrod Academic Library
California Institute of the Arts
24700 McBean Parkway
Valcencia, CA 91355
805-255-1050

Capacity: Lotus Spreadsheet: 2048 rows by 256 columns
Symphony Spreadsheet: 8194 rows by 256 columns

Description: *Lotus* has three major functions: spreadsheet, information management, and graphics. Does *not* have word processing, so users must find separate word processing package or purchase *Symphony* (described below). Major function of *1-2-3* is the spreadsheet; all other components are subordinate and unable to function without it. For example, information manager (not database manager), using essentially the same spreadsheet grid, uses data from the spreadsheet, and graphics system captures and also uses data from the spreadsheet.

System comes with six-lesson tutorial which covers all major functions, making start-up uncomplicated even for novice. Speed of computation or recalculation of this assembly-language program is fast. Also comes with extensive online help. *Lotus* has five basic charts: bar, stacked bar, side-by-side bar, pie, and scatter. Created with a simple/G, a great advantage over earlier and less sophisticated spreadsheets, such as *VisiCalc.* Essentially, all operation modes may be carried out with same command structure.

Symphony, an upgraded version of *Lotus,* adds telecommunications, word processing, a more potent database, and window management system.

Documentation: Over 350 pages of in-depth coverage of many areas. Other books also cover both *Lotus* and *Symphony,* and users may wish to consult them both before and after purchase. Two of these are *Inside Symphony,* an online tutorial with preformatted templates for immediate hands-on experience (Hayden, $49.94), and *Lotus 1-2-3,* a flipchart reference guide (Microref, $19.95).

Additional
information: Baras, Edward M. *Guide to Using Lotus 1-2-3.* McGraw-Hill, 1984.

Baras, Edward M. *The Symphony Book.* McGraw-Hill, 1985.

Cobb, Douglass. *Mastering Symphony.* Sybex, 1984. $14.95.

Name: **PFS Family**

Program type: Integrated software

Vendor: Software Publishing Corporation

Cost: Prices vary from $95 to $175 per module, depending upon program and microcomputer.

Hardware
requirements: Components of this integrated system will work with many microcomputers, but compatibility varies. Some modules will work with Apple II+, but many new versions will work only on a IIe or IIc with 128K. *PFS* also comes in a version for the Macintosh, Commodore 64, IBM PC, (XT, AT, jr.), Eagle, Compaq, TI Professional, and others. Latest version *(PFS:File, Report, and Write)* also supports Apple ProDOS operating system. There are so many variations and configurations that a prospective buyer should check with the vendor or write the manufacturer for current specifications.

Description: *PFS* (Personal Filing System) is a software family that began as a database system, but was gradually improved and expanded and now includes seven components: a word processor, speller, database management system (2 separate programs), spreadsheet, graphics package, and online utility, all of which may be purchased separately. All are easy to learn. They are integrated in several ways, not the least of which are command structures—learn one structure and much of it carries over to the others.

The word processor and file manager can produce personalized form letters. Graphics, produced with *PFS: Graph,* may be transferred to the word processor to include pie charts and tabular summaries in reports—in full color, if desired (if color printer is available). Spreadsheet statistics may also be moved to the word processor, making the total package very impressive, flexible, and professional. *PFS-Access* allows transmittal of these data over the phone lines.

PFS family of software is highly recommended by many librarians who use it, and it is widely used. *PFS:Proof,* an excellent spelling verification program, contains a dictionary of over 100,000 words. One difficulty is that the PFS database management system requires two modules both to file material and format the data into a printed tabular report (not the best sort of integration).

Documentation: All *PFS* software is well documented, with clear, easy-to-understand manuals.

Related
programs: Library templates are available for use with *PFS,* including *Library MicroTools: Overdues (*K–12 Micro-Media), for $49 (plus 5 percent shipping and handling). This template will generate reports by student, teacher, grade, notices, or title searches. Fields also include call number, due date, price, and comment.

Disk-based tutorial includes sample files.

Additional
information: Leonis, Ted. *Software Master for PFS: The Ultimate User's Guide.* Warner Books, 1984. $14.95.

Interlibrary Loan

Introduction

Two basic interlibrary loan functions may be automated with a microcomputer: generating request forms and transmitting the data to a network or microcomputer system such as a bulletin board system. *FILLS* performs both of these functions very well.

Reviews

FILLS (Fast Interlibrary Loan System) 2.0

Name:	**FILLS** (Fast Interlibrary Loan System) 2.0
Program type:	Interlibrary loan
Vendor:	MacNeal Memorial Hospital
Cost:	$360 (license for use on 1 microcomputer only), $430 with *Easy Link*
Hardware requirements:	IBM PC, XT, or AT, 64K; two disk drives; printer
Used at:	Health Sciences Library Danbury Hospital 24 Hospital Ave. Danbury, CT 06810 203-797-7279
Capacity:	3200 periodical titles

Description: This menu-driven program reduces the work in preparing special pin-feed ALA interlibrary loan forms (reports indicate from 40 to 60%). *FILLS* may be used with *Easy Link* to send requests, since it will not send requests by itself. Documentation has a chapter on using other telecommunications software (e.g., *Smartcom, PC Talk* or *Crosstalk*) to do so. *FILLS* also generates statistical reports, including time between original entry and final disposition, total cost, libraries from which materials were borrowed, and frequency of borrowed materials. *FILLS* form is displayed on screen and filled in by user. Great advantage of *FILLS* is that subsequent requests from a library or for a title can be answered by recalling information from stored request by number; data will be filled in by computer program. Nine reports are available: alphabetical periodical title lists, alphabetical library address lists, number of requests per periodical title, total cost charged per periodical title, number of requests per library, average return time per library, percentage fill rate per library, total average costs charged per library, and outstanding loan reports.

Even after all information has been entered, any datum can be changed. Requests may be printed, then sent via electronic mail, or printed and sent to a file for later Email transmission as part of a batch. Program reports with particular file (e.g., history) is nearly full, and report program must be run to clear it. Once transmitted, requests may be deleted from system. Capacity for outstanding loans (on double-side disk) is 400, or 2000 with IBM XT or AT; so it is important to record returned loans regularly to free up disk space. Loans may be sent to another library, filled, or canceled. Mailing labels may be generated.

Program produces special lists: alphabetical periodical list of all titles library has requested (periodical title information for up to 1000 periodicals per double-side disk [3200 on XT] is saved and each request is given a number; subsequent requests may be entered with code number); addresses of all libraries borrowed from; and numerical list of departments (15 spaces each) for which interlibrary loan requests have been made.

Installation is relatively easy, but users of version 1.0 must "redo" library and periodical files (fortunately, this is not time consuming or difficult).

Documentation: Excellent manual with extensive and easy-to-follow instructions for installation and procedures—complete walkthrough for entire system. Contains sample *FILLS*-generated reports.

Additional
information: Ben-Shir, Rya. "Fast Inter-Library Loans and Statistics," *American Libraries*, June 1984, p. 454.

Ben-Shir, Rya. "Fast Inter-Library Loans and Statistics: The Second, Enhanced Release," *Library Software Review*, May–June 1985, p. 132.

Miscellaneous Programs

Introduction

Software in this category do not fit easily into any other, since for the most part, they consist of templates, which require other software to run. A template is a model which has been created for use with a word processor, spreadsheet, or database manager to solve a general problem, after which it may be used, and altered, by others. For instance, a form letter may be created by using *AppleWorks*. Anyone who uses that same form may change the name and address, or any part of the letter, to meet his or her needs, and then print a new letter. An empty balance sheet for a school or library fiscal year may be created, then used by many schools or libraries; each fills in new, unique data, altering the sheet as required. Database management systems such as *dBase* may use a template to create a mailing list or other tool. In short, a template is created when work created for one job is used for another—a blank form, to be filled in over and over again.

Sources of Additional Information

Library Template Exchange (Robert Skapura), 1920 Monument Blvd., Suite 540, Concord, CA 94520.

Reviews

AlphaChart

AppleWorks for School Librarians

Library MicroTools: Overdues

Shelving Books the LC Way

Templates–DB Master

Templates–VisiCalc

Name:	**AlphaChart**
Program type:	Graphics (charts)
Vendor:	Spectral Graphics Software
Cost:	$29.95
Hardware requirements:	Apple II series
Description:	This incredibly easy-to-use program will produce professional graphics in record time. Graphic depictions of budgets, circulation comparisons, sources of income, and other library statistics will help enliven a word-processed report. Bar and pie charts are supported, in various colors (user or auto-fill) and sizes, and user-entered text may be placed anywhere on the charts by a sometimes awkward (though wholly adequate) editor. Charts may be one-, two-, or three-dimensional, and be printed out or saved to disk for future editing and use. Program also supports user drawing of boxes, circles, dots, lines, and other shapes, as well as figure enlargement or reduction.
Documentation:	Twelve-page booklet has many examples of charts, as well as simple step-by-step directions.

Name:	**AppleWorks for School Librarians**
Program type:	Template/book package
Vendor:	Hi Willow Research & Publishing Co.
Cost:	$20 for book and templates; multiple copies of book without template disk are $10 each.
Hardware requirements:	Apple II series with *AppleWorks*, and 128K
Description:	This template/tutorial book/disk package has eight sections: Introduction to *AppleWorks;* Word Processor, Data Base; Spreadsheet; Cut and Paste (moving text or material from one part of document to another); Utilization of *AppleWorks;* Collection Mapping; and Curriculum Mapping. Indexed, step-by-step explanation and guide to *AppleWorks,* and much more. Exercises, ex-

amples, command summaries, and planning are major teaching-style components. Advanced features are clearly outlined and defined: using tabs, printer options, Boolean searching in database mode, splitting the spreadsheet, etc. For instance, examples illustrate use of database component to create acquisitions file; spreadsheet is shown to be helpful in analyzing library media use and budget; cut-and-paste functions include transfer of data files between two databases, between two spreadsheet files, from database file to word processor file, and from spreadsheet file to word processor file. In addition to book (which is well worth the modest purchase price), disk is well integrated with book and brings whole package to life, besides many templates and boilerplate files used in teaching. Collection mapping techniques are useful for building stronger book collection, as well as advice for integrating the budgeting process into this system.

Name:	**Library MicroTools: Overdues**
Program type:	Template
Vendor:	K–12 MicroMedia
Cost:	$49 (plus 5% shipping and handling)
Hardware requirements:	Apple II series
Capacity:	500 records per disk
Description:	Single-program overlay or template for *PFS:File* and *PFS:Report,* which are part of *PFS* family of integrated software. Once data are entered, system will generate reports by student, teacher, grade, notices, and title searches. Format provides for nine categories of information: teacher, student, grade, title, author, call number, date due, price, and comment.
Documentation:	Disk-based tutorial

Name:	**Shelving Books the LC Way: A Self-Test**
Program type:	Employee training

Vendor:	Southwestern Oregon Community College
Cost:	Consult vendor. Program will be customized for any other call numbers for additional $30.
Hardware requirements:	Apple II series
Description:	Staff examination program, designed to test employees on shelving books by Library of Congress Classification on five levels, *after* it has been taught by traditional methods (though it provides practice as well). Operation is simple: program records student's name and date, then tests on level 1 and progresses through level 5. Each level has five sets of five call numbers. Five books, represented in high-resolution graphics, are used in each trial; call numbers are on spine of each book; books are then "shelved" in proper order, left to right, by selecting correct identifier (1 through 5) for each book. As much practice as desired is allowed at each level. Student's name, date, and progress at each level are printed automatically (if printer is available).
Documentation:	Six pages, with list of all call number sets.

Name:	**Templates—DB Master**
Program type:	Templates
Vendor:	Micro Libraries
Cost:	$7.50 per disk
Hardware requirements:	Apple II series
Description:	This series of templates makes it possible to load in form or worksheet for database management with *DB Master* and begin work immediately, without constructing complicated, difficult equations often associated with such work. Some templates are

> *Microcomputer Software Collection:* Simple microcomputer software catalog with two subject fields
>
> *AV Equipment Inventory:* Has fields for bulbs and repair history

Film Booking: Tracks films booked from various sources

Overdues: Valid fields include name, grade, call number, title, date due, and price

Periodicals: Title, number of issues/year, print, fiche/film, subject, location

Other templates: *Special Talent Class,* book order, and deposition transcripts (to index testimony)

Documentation: Self-documenting

Name: **Templates — VisiCalc**

Program type: Template

Vendor: Micro Libraries (Eric Anderson)

Cost: $5 per disk for *VisiCalc* templates; $7.50 per disk for *DB Master* templates

Hardware requirements: Apple II series.

Description: These templates constitute preprogrammed worksheets for *VisiCalc,* a powerful spreadsheet (no longer published, but owned and used by many libraries and individuals). They may be used with *AppleWorks* after conversion to ProDOS files. Some of the templates for *VisiCalc* are

Circulation Statistics #1: Designed for daily circulation, with rows for days, columns for material type

Circulation Statistics #2: Designed to handle print and nonprint circulation

Budget #1: For department ordering; columns for departments and rows for type of expenditure

Budget #2: For yearly departmental use; high school departmentalized budget system; computer scheduling

Budget #3: For journal-type high school expenditure records

Budget #4: High school library budget templates

Budget #5: District-wide budget, with New York subcategories

Budget #6: High school building level budget, with New York subcategories

Catalog Statistics

Computer Reservations

Assorted Statistics

Downtime Statistics: To calculate computer downtime

Student Wage: To figure student help wages in library

Statistics–OCLC: To track OCLC activity

Documentation: Self-documenting

Public Relations

Introduction

A very useful function of the microcomputer is to improve the public image of the library by relieving librarians of much tedious work associated with traditional public relations. Hand-made signs may be eliminated.

Some of the things which the software will prepare include

Badges and name tags   Letterheads
Banners   Newsletters
Bumper stickers   Puzzles (crosswords, word-
Greeting cards and announcements   finds, mazes)
Iron-on T-shirt transfers   Signs

The most impressive aspect to all this is that just about anyone can make exciting and useful material on the first try.

Sources of Additional Information

Rappaport, Susan. "Computer Graphics for the Novice," *Library Journal,* September 1, 1986, p. 146.
Schmeltz, Leslie R. *"Print Shop* and *Newsroom,"Nibble,* March 1986, p. 82.

Reviews

Art Studio

Newsroom and Clip Art

Prince

Print Shop

Name: **Art Studio**

Program type: Graphics

Vendor: Spectrum HoloByte, Inc.

Cost: $49.50 (plus $2.50 shipping and handling)

Hardware
requirements: IBM PC, 128K; dot matrix printer

Description: This package—perhaps the IBM answer to MacPaint—is very good, but does not have quite the power. Easy to use, including the drawing of radial lines, boxes, erasing, sketching, consecutive boxes, marking with patterns, making arcs, circles, concentric circles, ellipses, and cut and paste. Nine type fonts are supported, as well as a batch of icon fonts, which give each key on keyboard a different symbol or picture (a hammer, drawing of North America, boat, person, etc.). Another font automatically produces arrows in all shapes and pointing in all directions. "Screen capture" enhancement integrates *Art Studio* with such programs as *Lotus 1-2-3* or *PFS:Graph*. By loading in "capture" first, up to nine screens (per boot) may be captured for *Art Studio* editing.

Documentation: Ninety-five–page indexed booklet gives complete instructions for operating the system, including tips, tools, etc. Five appendixes explain type fonts, backgrounds, making backups, and advanced applications such as high resolution, custom brush, printer drivers, and screen capture.

Name: **Newsroom** and **Clip Art**

Program type: Graphics/public relations

Vendor: Springboard Software, Inc.

Cost: $49.95, *Newsroom*
$29.95, *Clip Art Volume 1*
$39.95, *Clip Art Volume 2 (Business)*

Hardware
requirements: Apple II series; IBM PC, PCjr; Commodore 64; dot
matrix printer

Description: This newsletter produces quality, two-column newsletter
pages, complete with clip art. If *Clip Art* volume is also
purchased, 1200 designs are available. *Clip Art Volume
2* contains over 800 additional pieces and artwork
suitable for business advertising (realty, industry, office,
shopping, graphs, charts, etc.). Operation of this icon-
driven program is simple, though at times cumbersome,
since pages must be prepared one "panel" at a time (there
are 6, 8, or 10 panels per page, depending upon whether
a banner is used or page is 11 or 14 inches long). Takes
quite some time to "come to grips" with system; one
must first take "photos" of clip art, prepare text, lay out
pages, select correct-size font, etc. Then, however, it is
easier to produce newsletter.

All but amazing is program's ability to "wrap"
prepared text around any piece of clip art; if clip art is
rearranged, text rearranges itself accordingly. Work is
modularized (i.e., copy is typed in copy area, graphics
are made or selected with editor, banner is produced in
banner department, or finished text is "zapped" cross
country with telecommunications feature. Program also
produces spectacular flyers or banners for many types
of work.

Documentation: Packages come with catalog of all clip art and complete
instructions for using programs.

Name: **Prince**

Program type: Graphics

Vendor: Baudville

Cost: $69.95

Hardware
requirements: Apple II series; dot matrix printer (Epson Style or C.
Itoh Style – specify type)

Description: Program performs several unique functions: captures
screen images, makes heat-transfer patterns for T-shirts

and bumper stickers. Does not come with large picture library, but image may be created by user or "captured" from other programs (some compatible programs are listed below). *Prince* excels at printing greeting cards (somewhat different in design from *Print Shop*), signs, letterheads, name tags, and will even create stuffed toys (it makes the outlines; you have to stuff toys yourself), and manual has many other suggestions. System's four color ribbons contain heat-transfer ink (ordinary multi-color ribbons won't do same job). Pictures on screen may be adjusted in color as desired (it helps, therefore, to have color monitor). Once created, pictures may also be "stretched", "flattened," or repeated. "Frozen" picture is then printed one color at a time. Disk tutorial has several ready-to-go sample pictures on reverse side. Pictures may be printed in three sizes: small, medium, large; and new pictures may be saved on data disk. If only one color, up to 99 copies may be made in one run.

Prince is compatible with otner graphics programs, such as *Blazing Paddles* (illustrator), *Pixit* (graphics processor for creating shapes, shape table, and high-resolution pictures), *Dazzle Draw,* and *Micro Illustrator* (all Baudville products). Shape libraries are supplied (separately), by Baudville.

Documentation: Thirty-page manual, with complete instructions, has illustrations and examples. Basic procedures are covered, as are tips and troubleshooting, how to change ribbon cartridges, and how to handle various printers.

Name:	**Print Shop**
Program type:	Graphics/public relations
Vendor:	Broderbund Software, Inc.
Cost:	$49.95; $59.95 for IBM PC XT, PCjr. version $79.95 Apple Macintosh
Hardware requirements:	Apple II series; Commodore 64; IBM PC XT, PCjr. Dot matrix printer/graphics required (will work with most

dot matrix printers). Macintosh needs 512K with *Image-writer* or *Laserwriter* (or compatable).

Used at: Winthrop College Library
Rock Hill, SC 29733
803-323-2131

Description: Easy way to prepare customized greeting cards, posters, flyers, banners, and letterheads. Package comes ready to use, with dozens of pieces of clip art that may be arranged in patterns in small, medium, or large size. Letter types vary from block and technical to newspaper headline, may easily be centered or arranged creatively on page, in 3-D, outline, or solid. Easy to use, program does fully professional job, producing copy which formerly could be generated only by typesetter or graphics artist.

Other uses reported by libraries include shelf-end labels (call-number signs), invitations, and greeting cards. Special "Screen Magic" feature permits printing high-resolution images which have been created and saved with any other graphics system. *Print Shop Paper Pack* has 120 sheets of assorted, brightly colored paper for signs and posters produced with *Print Shop*.

Documentation: Booklet, with all clip art illustrated and numbered, makes it easy to select artwork without consulting all pictures on disk.

Related
programs: *Print Shop Companion* has additional type styles, boarders, custom calendar, and graphics editor. (Apple II series, 64K, only; $39.95).

Print Shop Graphics Library 1 and *2* enhance *Print Shop* ($24.95 Apple; $34.95 IBM PC XT, PCjr.; disk 2 available only in Apple version) with several hundred additional designs.

Graphics Expander Volume 1 (Springboard Software, Inc.; $39.95) has 300 new graphics, and drawing and editing tools, for *Print Shop* (for use with Apple II series, 64K).

Print Master (Unison World; $59.95), another excellent graphics package (similar to *Print Shop*), has 122 designs. Auxiliary package, *Art Gallery I,* has 140 additional graphics (IBM only).

Certificate Maker (Springboard Software, Inc.; $49.95, Apple II series, Commodore 64/128; $59.95, IBM) provides more than 200 certificates in many categories for custom printing. Choose from a variety of type styles, sizes, signature and date lines.

Additional
information: Everhart, Nancy, and Claire Hartz. "Creating Graphics with *The Print Shop*," *Library Journal*, May 1985, p. 118.

Ridgeway, Trish. "*The Print Shop*: A Review," *Apple Library User's Group Newsletter*, December 1984, p. 20.

Serials Control

Introduction

The control of serials has long been difficult, but the software in this chapter helps keep track of materials as they arrive at the library. Some provide such "extras" as routing slips, claim notices, and the like.

Reviews

Mag-it
Serial Control System

Name:	**Mag-it**
Program type:	Serials
Vendor:	Right On Programs
Cost:	$50
Hardware requirements:	Apple II series; IBM PC, XT, PCjr.; Commodore 64, 128
Capacity:	Unknown
Description:	Central virtue of this program is ease of use; just pop in diskette and you are off and running with automated magazine holdings list which is excellent for small school libraries. Maintained data include magazine in-

formation, publisher information, supplier information, number of missing issues (up to 25), and missing-issue information. Entries may be searched by title or publisher, and added or deleted. Complete listing of titles may be printed, as well as mailing labels for tracking missing issues. Allows easy data correction; if entry is incorrect, only the specific line need be altered.

Documentation: Two pages give basic details of program operation

Name: **Serial Control System**

Program type: Serial control

Vendor: Professional Software

Cost: $900, check-in/claiming/renewal (this module is base package)
$400, holdings list
$300, bindery management
$700, routing
$100, hospital library preloaded data
$75, "Demo Pak" ($65 credit toward full system)

Hardware requirements: IBM PC, XT, AT; 132-column printer

Capacity: 600 subscriptions if two drives are used; more subscriptions require hard disk ·

Description: This menu-driven program, which maintains control over large number of subscriptions, is generally suited to hospital or special libraries. Subscription data may be accessed by title (first 8 letters of name). Automatically relates most issues to internal calendar, based upon issue-date entry. To use claiming, expiration, and renewal functions, it is necessary to enter title, frequency (weekly, monthly, etc.), issue numbering scheme, starting volume/issue number of current subscription, and number of copies expected for each issue. Based upon these data, system can produce receipt cards, claim reports, and report on subscription expirations. List of currently missing issues can also be produced.

This highly sophisticated system can delay a

periodical on claiming list until specified grace period expires. Further, system incorporates bibliographic database which allows descriptions of any length, who subscribes to what, etc. Greatest hurdle in getting system up and running is "load sheets." Moreover, users must be prepared for time-consuming initial data entry. System uses department file, serial description file, and subscription file. Thus data are linked together for sophisticated sorting and reports.

Documentation: Several hundred pages (in looseleaf binder) give start-up instructions, management details, use with hard disk, etc.

Spreadsheets and Statistics

Introduction

A spreadsheet is the computer version of an accountant's paper and pencil. With such an "intelligent" adjunct, it is possible to construct a balance or other statistical form which calculates automatically. An electronic spreadsheet is "layered," with the "bottom" layer containing user-supplied instructions which tell the computer to add, subtract, multiply, divide—or perform just about any calculation on data in specified squares. Balance sheets or other statistical forms may also be printed out, with new data each time, for hardcopy, or simply recalculated for screen viewing. Recalculation is the real miracle of the electronic spreadsheet. The contents of each square, either the data or the formulas, may be changed at any time. All contingent totals are instantly changed by the program, which is why spreadsheets have been labeled "What If?" systems. Users may examine the consequences of a large number of choices quickly—which would take someone with pencil and paper, or even an adding machine, a much longer time. Spreadsheets are excellent for library work, especially the budgeting/planning process.

However, such systems can take quite some time to learn, but, once learned, they can become one's greatest ally, making otherwise difficult calculations easy and rewarding. Fortunately, there are short cuts, called "templates," or spreadsheets with formulas that have already been created. Some are free and some are for sale. There are many about, and some sources are listed below. They are loaded into the main program quickly and easily, at which point the user need only enter the raw data.

VisiCalc was the first major spreadsheet, and it has maintained its popularity for many years. It was purchased by another company and then discontinued. Nevertheless, many people, including librarians, still use it; so templates are included in this volume.

Selection Guidelines

It can be difficult to determine whether one spreadsheet is better than another, without trying them out or consulting people who have used them. Some basic criteria which should be considered are "windows" (some newer spreadsheets use excellent pull-down windows), printing (some spreadsheets have limited printout capability), online help screens, cursor movement, capacity, and calculation speed.

In addition to spreadsheets, there are other specially designed statistical programs to aid librarians. Two of these are *OutputM* and *Create*.

Sources of Additional Information

Clark, Philip M. *Microcomputer Spreadsheet Models for Libraries.* ALA, 1985.

Henderson, Thomas B., et al. *Spreadsheet Software from VisiCalc to 1-2-3.* Que, 1983.

Saffady, William. "Electronic Spreadsheets and Data Management Software for Libraries," *Library Technology Reports,* July–August 1984.

Swersey, Patricia Johnson. "Jogging Your Memory – Using Spreadsheets Effectively," *Library Software Review,* January–February 1986, p. 25.

Reviews

Create

Legerit

MultiPlan

OutputM

SuperCalc

Name:	**Create**
Program type:	Statistical (reference) surveys
Vendor:	Microdex
Cost:	$80
Hardware requirements:	Apple II series; IBM PC, XT; or compatibles

Description: With this "authoring" system, user creates customized database management program for statistical reports and tallies, as well as analyses of survey material. Its use is rather straightforward, but it is not bug-free. Users must have initialized data disk, and once the program has been created, it is independent of master program disk. Users may choose from a number of predetermined fields, or select new fields of their choice. Typical data that program will track include day of week and time that data were collected, length of transaction, type of location, person who took survey, reference sources or books, subject category, and whether survey was made by phone, in person, or by mail. Surveys may be completed on paper, then input into program for analysis. It is easy to "bomb" the program, however—at least before the "bugs" are discovered. Some input data are not immediately clear (e.g., trying to input date can drive you crazy), but this is minor complaint and does not interfere with utility of program. Statistics in all fields may be generated as two-dimensional frequency tables.

Documentation: Booklet has hints on sampling techniques and many forms to help design *Create* programs.

Additional
information: Smith, Dana E. "Customized Reference Statistics Programs," *American Libraries,* March 1984, p. 179.

Name: **Ledgerit**

Program type: Order file

Vendor: Right On Programs

Cost: $50

Hardware
requirements: Apple II series; Commodore PET, 64; IBM PC, XT, PCjr.

Capacity: Unknown

Description: This easy-to-use program maintains simple book order file and tracks expenditures. Allows users to type in titles and encumber whatever list price is required, then enter actual price and date of delivery, when item is received. All budget entries may be coded for easy access. Excellent for small library.

Documentation: Short booklet

Name: **MultiPlan**

Program type: Database management

Vendor: Microsoft Corp.

Cost: $250

Hardware
requirements: PC DOS, CP/M operating systems. Versions available for most microcomputers. 64K minimum RAM

Capacity: 254 rows, 63 columns

Description: There are cosmetic as well as significant differences between *Multiplan* and *VisiCalc* and other worksheets; most noticeable is the way cells are labeled: numbers are used for rows and columns in *MultiPlan,* instead of numbers and letters as in *VisiCalc. MultiPlan* is also more nearly menu driven.

Two command lines initiate most major functions associated with spreadsheets. Commands are used directly, without a prompt (usually "/" is needed in *VisiCalc* before command can be invoked). Users simply type in first letter of any command in menu (at bottom of screen). This makes it much easier for first-time users to get started in *MultiPlan,* compared with more cryptic spreadsheets.

Also shows percentage of worksheet storage space remaining and worksheet name. Special function is that *VisiCalc* users can move their files directly into *Multi-Plan.* "Help" file, summoned by "H" (at any time), relates information about command or function currently in use.

Documentation: Extensive manual and reference card

Name:	**OutputM**
Program type:	Output measures recordkeeping
Vendor:	Center for the Study of Rural Librarianship (program was funded by LSCA and developed with Library Development Division, State of Pennsylvania)
Cost:	$99. May be examined for $15 (applicable toward purchase)
Hardware requirements:	IBM PC, XT; Columbia; 128K
Description:	Basic function is to automate tabulation of the nine library outputs: circulation per capita, in-library use of materials, library visits per capita, reference transactions per capita, program attendance per capita, reference fill rate, title fill rate, browsers fill rate, and registration as percentage of population. Designed for all types and sizes, program can handle data for five districts, each with 50 member libraries or 250 total. Data may be stored 1 to 10 years. Statistical calculations include average data for one or all libraries.
	Program stores annual circulation data, jurisdiction population, annual in-library material use, annual library visits, annual program attendance, annual reference transactions (number and completions), titles sought and found, subjects and authors sought and found, browsers' finds, number of browsers, library registrations, households in jurisdiction, holdings, requests immediately unavailable and requests available in 7 days and 30 days. Sample file facilitates learning program. From main menu, users may initialize (create) a new file, assign names to districts or libraries, enter or examine library data, summarize, or exit. Summarizing feature produces either total or average amounts for 20 transactions and services above.
Documentation:	Twenty-page accompanying document covers starting sample file, and backing up diskettes. Installation procedures for hard or floppy disk are clearly outlined.
Additional information:	"*OutputM* Simplifies Output Measures Record Keeping," *American Libraries,* December 1984, p. 830.

Name:	**SuperCalc**
Program type:	Spreadsheet
Vendor:	Sorcim Corporation
Cost:	*SuperCalc3,* V.2.1, $395 (IBM PC)
	SuperCalc3, $195 (PCjr.)
	SuperCalc3a, $195 (Apple)
	SuperCalc2, $295
	SuperCalc, $195

Hardware requirements: Because *SuperCalc* will run in CP/M or MSDOS form, is available for many types of microcomputers, including most majors: Apple, IBM PC, Radio Shack (model II).

Capacity: *SuperCalc3* allows up to 9999 rows, 127 columns

Description: Three versions of *SuperCalc* provide increasingly advanced sophistication and power. Unlike *VisiCalc,* its grid of rows and columns may be removed, if desired. Because *SuperCalc* will print out grid, necessary to turn it off before printing, if report without lines is desired. Other important features are ability to treat text as values and text formulas as part of conditional tests. Special commands, such as "Lookup" and "Sort," give it tremendous powers, some of which are associated only with database management.

Despite these improvements over *VisiCalc, SuperCalc* is criticized by spreadsheet users as much slower in operation. *SuperCalc* is faster in other ways, however. It will, at one time, format entire range of cells, rows, columns, or whole spreadsheet, instead of just one cell, as does *VisiCalc.* Possible formats include integer, dollars and cents, bar graph, text left or right, exponent, and general default format (to 4 decimal places). Entries or cells may be "protected" (locked) in *SuperCalc,* making it impossible to make a change by accident. Simple program may be created (execute function or macro), instead of typing long string of commands into keyboard.

SuperCalc has too many features to detail here, but they include protection against overwriting files already on disk, file compatibility with *WordStar* or any CP/M word processor, file security with special "Hide" command, and file interchange with *VisiCalc*. *Super-Calc* can also use Sorcim's *SuperData Interchange (SDI)*. *SuperCalc*'s help file may by summoned at any time by typing "?" for pertinent assistance.

SuperCalc3, version 2.1, is incredible worksheet, with integrated database management, graphics, Fast-Math (special feature that speeds calculation), and Sideways (horizontal printing program). Users have access to immense calculating power (*SuperCalc3* will support up to 8 megabytes of memory with Intel's *Above Board*) and high-quality color graphics (including pie and bar and line charts). Difficult to imagine a library which needs more number-crunching.

Documentation: Excellent manual with step-by-step instructions and help. Other books, such as Clark's (see below), are also good, and perhaps better for librarian than the documentation.

Related programs: Sorcim's line of related, compatible products includes *SuperWriter*, a word processing program

Additional information: Clark, Philip M. *Microcomputer Spreadsheet Models for Libraries*. American Library Association, 1985. This book is good recommendation for *SuperCalc,* since it not only serves as general introduction to spreadsheets (with comparison of 5 popular programs) but also contains 57 templates based on *SuperCalc* for library use. These templates cover all bases—from budgets, expenditures, and activity summaries to output measures.

Training Programs

Introduction

There are programs, sometimes called "tutorials," which teach people how to use programs. Often, a major program will provide its own online tutorial (or at least online help files), but more often it will not. Much time can be saved learning to use such programs as *WordStar, dBase,* and *VisiCalc* if a training program is purchased. These come in several forms—some good, some bad. Occasionally, they come with audiotapes to provide a step-by-step talkthrough for the user. Nearly always, they come with a manual and one or more diskettes (which require ownership of the program to yield full benefit).

Other types of tutorials provide training in use of the computer itself, rather than a particular program, or in use of an operating system or programming language, such as Basic or Pascal.

Below are a few of the best tutorials, but many other exist—far more than can be reviewed in this book. Consult the article cited below for more programs.

Sources of Additional Information

Exner, Ron. "Do-It-Yourself Computer Training," *Popular Computing,* mid-October 1984, p. 129. This article lists several dozen suppliers of training software

Reviews

Sudden Knowledge Training Programs
Inside Symphony

Name: **Sudden Knowledge Training Programs**

Program type: Training program

Vendor: Cdex Intelligence Corporation

Cost: $99.95 to $149.95

Hardware
requirements: Apple II/III series; IBM PC; Tandy 2000; Texas Instruments Professional

Description: Cdex has most varied and best-developed training programs, and its software packages are too numerous to
list. They cover use of the various computers (Apple,
IBM PC, Tandy 2000, Texas Instruments Professional)
and, depending upon the type of computer, may cover
*CP/M, dBase, Lotus, Symphony, Communications,
General Ledger* programs, *SuperCalc,* and many more.

The bulk of programs, however, is for the IBM
PC and compatibles. Subjects include *MultiPlan, Peach-
tree Accounting, VisiCalc, Symphony, WordStar, dBase
II/III, PC DOS, SuperCalc,* etc.

The next largest number of programs is for the
Apple II series (only one program is listed for the Apple
III, *Cdex Training for the BPI General Accounting
Program*).

Fewer programs still are listed for Texas Instruments, and only four for the Tandy 2000 (for *Lotus*
business functions). Besides, these programs are im-
plicitly or explicitly business oriented (e.g., *Analyzing
Sales Performance with the VisiCalc Program, Making
Key Business Decisions with SuperCalc,* and *Making
Key Business Decisions with Lotus 1-2-3*).

Cdex programs are easy to use, generally as
lessons, and function with or without the programs.
Sometimes we begin to feel as if just screens of data are
being fed to us, but finally they assume an interactive
technique, often encouraging users to work out some
problem and relying on the only tried-and-true method,
"learning by doing." To get the most out of this, you
need to own *SuperCalc* or *MultiPlan,* or whatever program is taught, for only then will you experience an actual step-by-step tutorial. If you are going to take *dBase*
or *WordStar* seriously, Cdex is all but required. It will
save you many hours (if not days) of groping in the dark.

Documentation: Most Cdex programs come with a short manual.

Name:	**Inside Symphony**
Program type:	Tutorial
Vendor:	Hayden Book Co.
Cost:	$49.95
Hardware requirements:	IBM PC, XT, or compatible, with 384K minimum; 2 disk drives; and *Symphony* package
Description:	Series of tutorials for exciting major software packages (*Inside Symphony* is reviewed here as example). *Symphony* module contains extensive manual with lessons, user's reference guide, and diskette of templates, useful both in themselves and in teaching how to use *Symphony*. Templates include *Sales Analysis, Project Management, Product Income and Expense, Project Plan, Personal Net Worth, Condominium Monthly Report,* and *Employee Bonus. Symphony* training package book centers around communications, database, DOS, graphics, keyboard/special keys, macros, spreadsheets, windows, word processing, and working with *Symphony,* as well as printouts of eight spreadsheet templates. First part of each section is walkthrough of main commands, followed by practice exercises. Well-done lessons provide much practice in basic functions of *Symphony*. Coordinated with practice exercises is "Performance Aids": step-by-step keyboard instructions for specific actions. To use communications function (for example), "Performance Aid 2" delineates three preparatory steps, eight protocol steps, six steps for entering number to dial, and so on. Like tutor sitting by your side as you work.
Documentation:	Programs come with manual of more than 200 pages of step-by-step instructions. Separate "User's Reference Guide" is speedy way to find help with just about any part of *Symphony* (including templates on the disk).

Utilities

Introduction

"Utilities" are housekeeping programs which allow control over other programs or data files. Typical utilities are copy programs, catalog management, and memory usage. Of these, copy programs have always been the most useful and popular. When microcomputers first became stylish, one could backup (or copy) 80 percent of all copy-protected programs by using *Locksmith*. Today, the many new copy programs and methods include *Essential Data Duplicator* and *Copy II+*, and "copy cards" (hardware components), which allow the computer to take a "snapshot" of any program in memory. But even with these aids, it has become difficult to copy some diskettes with *any* program. The primary reason is that copy-protection schemes have become more sophisticated (it is also possible to purchase a copy-protection program, in the event you want to protect your software from pirates). Some schemes now randomize the parameters for each copy of a program, and *Locksmith* parameters, even if known, may be worthless, because each program requires a unique set of parameters. Only programs which are completely resident in memory ("total load") can be duplicated successfully with a "copy card." In the end, a device either copies in a straightforward manner or a large investment in time is required. Fiddling with parameters or attempting to "crack" a program often takes more time than librarians can (or should) spend on such a chore. As a result, we rely more and more on the warranty protection offered by the publisher. Usually, this means sending $5 or more to the manufacturer.

Copying or moving files for word processing, database management, or other uses can often be done with the program that creates them, but it may be slow. Bulk copy "file transfer" (such as *FID,* in the case of Apple) is much more efficient. The Apple *ProDOS File Management System* is a little more complicated, but accomplishes file transfer or copy needs, and formats disks as well.

With the Apple IIe computer, it is not always possible to use the full 128K RAM memory, since the computer addresses only 64K blocks at one time. *Extra K* will make up the difference by using all the memory (at least for some programs), and it has other advantages. For example, it allows two operating systems to reside in memory at the same time (essentially creating two Apples in one), and it increases the number of high-resolution screens in memory, making animation possible.

Sidekick provides IBM PC users with many features which should come with all computers, including a notepad, calendar, calculator, etc.

Sources of Additional Information

Garber, Marvin. "Copy Protection: How Good Is Good?" *Library Software Review,* 1985.

Planton, Stanley. "Hacking at the Apple Tree," *Library Journal,* November 1985, p. 156.

Also see *Hardcore Computist* (Box 110846-T, Tacoma, WA 98411), each issue of which has articles and hints for de-protecting many types of software. Of more benefit to users of public access software than library-specific software, and admittedly for the diehard.

Reviews

Copy II+

CopyWrite

Diversi-Copy

Essential Data Duplicator

Extra K

Pinpoint

SideKick

Name:	**Copy II+**
Program type:	Bit copy program
Vendor:	Central Point Software, Inc.
Cost:	$40
Hardware requirements:	Apple II series. (Copy II MAC is available for Macintosh; Copy II 64/128 for Commodore; Copy II PC for IBM PC, XT, and compatibles)

Used at: Sulzer Regional Library
4455 N. Lincoln
Chicago, IL 60625
Contact: Marvin Garber
312-728-8652

Description: Currently the ultimate copy program, in both ability and convenience. Will display catalog with file lengths, deleted files, or hidden characters; fix file sizes; undelete (provided files have been deleted from directory, not written over) or delete selected files, all files, or DOS. Files may be locked, unlocked, and renamed; disk catalog alphabetized; diskettes formatted; disk, files, or drive speed verified (also verify if two files are or are not identical); view files directly; draw track/sector map; work with sector editor (read, write to, or edit sector information, etc.); and change boot program.

Impressive as this sounds, major feature is bit copy routine, which comes with built-in parameters ("parms" [for short] are special codes needed to copy many protected programs). With this built-in feature, copying can begin immediately for many programs, without need to hunt down parameters (as with other programs). Unfortunately, not all of several hundred parameters work every time, since manufacturers continue to change them. This utility also conveniently converts DOS and ProDOS files and works with ProDOS Sider (hard disk) files.

Documentation: 120-page manual fully describes system. Appendix B, "Protection Schemes," gives advice on how to outwit manufacturers who do not want purchasers to make their own backups (making archival copies is perfectly legal).

Name: **CopyWrite**

Program type: Copy program

Vendor: Quaid Software Limited

Cost: $50 (No refunds!)

Hardware
requirements: IBM PC, XT, AT; 128K (does not run on IBM PCjr.). Compaq Portable, Deskpro, Zenith Z-150, Sperry PC,

Leading Edge, Panasonic Sr. Partner, Tandy 1200 HD, Tandy 1000 with DMA, and AT&T 6300. Only one drive required.

Description: Manufacturer would not send us a review copy, only literature. (Reason, according to letter, is that product is not copy protected.) According to literature, *CopyWrite* will make copies of wide range of IBM software, including business packages (among hundreds listed: *Framework, dBase III, VisiCalc*), and education/recreation packages (including *Adventure,* by Microsoft; *Sargon III, Starcross, Zork*). Since copy-protection schemes change almost by the minute, Quaid Software publishes new edition of its product each month, which may be purchased by owners of *CopyWrite* for $15. Publisher may be called for consultation regarding specific software before their system is purchased. Sounds good, and they seem confident.

Documentation: Unknown

Name: **Diversi-Copy**

Program type: Copy program

Vendor: Diversified Software Research, Inc.

Cost: $30. (This is known as "freeware": if you like it and want to use it, you must sent $30 to vendor. It is permitted to copy the program to give to friends, for which you may charge $5; but if they use it, they must also send $30.)

Hardware requirements: Apple II series, 48K

Description: Not a bit copier, but strictly for use as quick backup utility. Noteworthy because it is probably fastest backup copier around. On 128K machine, program will copy one disk in approximately 20 seconds. Will format disks at rate of 18 seconds per disk (requires extra 128K card for full disks). Will copy full disk on two-drive Apple in 33 seconds; will also copy for DOS 3.3, Pascal, CP/M, and ProDOS. If 200K (or close to it) is available, will "mass produce" diskettes by using RAM as pseudo-high-speed disk drive (i.e., RAM disk).

Copies produced as blank diskettes are fed into drive one after the other. System will operate with one or two drives, but much faster with two. Formatting does not produce bootable disks, only blank data disks. System will also check if two diskettes are identical. Interesting arcade game *Dogfight,* is included. Program does *not* backup copy-protected diskettes; strictly for use with unprotected disks.

Documentation: Self-documenting

Name: **Essential Data Duplicator**

Program type: Copy program

Vendor: Utilico Microware

Cost: $79.95

Hardware
requirements: Apple II series

Description: This heavy-duty copy program, in most respects like other programs in this chapter, is in some ways superior in that it provides extras, in addition to standard routine. One advantage is speed; it is probably the fastest bit copier. *Copy II+* usually takes 8 minutes (more or less, depending upon program), but *EDD* takes, on average, only 2½ minutes.

Documentation: Like every important copy program, *EDD* comes with list of parameters (special information which allows copy program to copy it) for many common programs. Few educational and library-specific programs are listed, since there is no great demand for them in the mass market. List is updated frequently and mailed to registered *EDD* purchasers bimonthly (if self-addressed, stamped envelope is sent in advance).

Name: **Extra K**

Program type: Utility

Vendor:	Beagle Bros. Micro Software, Inc.
Cost:	$39.95
Hardware requirements:	Apple II series, DOS 3.3 or ProDOS
Description:	Excellent memory utility makes full use of 128K of Apple IIe, but will not work with all programs. Other features come with program and are perhaps more useful:

Disk Compare, for comparing two disks for identical tracks and sectors

Disk Copy, fast program for copying diskettes in ProDOS, Pascal, or CP/M; will work with one or two drives

Disk Format, program for initializing ProDOS disks

Extra Apple, memory partition program. Each of two partitions may run under different operating system. Only one program may be run at one time, but you can switch back and forth between operating systems without rebooting. Works, however, only with programs that do not need auxiliary memory or need not be booted. Special program, *Transfer,* allows quick movement of programs between the two Apple partitions.

Extra Screen, allows large number of screen displays to be maintained in auxiliary memory for immediate viewing. Depending upon screen type (high or low resolution, etc.), 3 (double high-resolution graphics) to as many as 62 screen displays (40-column text or low-resolution graphics). This function permits animation.

Hybrid Create permits creation of dual-boot disk (i.e., disk that is half ProDOS and half DOS 3.3).

Spooler, for creating print buffer, works only with Apple IIc, using ProDOS 1.10 and printer in slot 1. Regrettably, this program will not work with word processors, but can print long program listings, freeing computer for other operations while printing continues.

Documentation:	Fifty-six–page booklet details each function

Name:	**Pinpoint** (Desktop Accessories for Apple II)

Program type:	Word processing utility
Vendor:	Pinpoint Publishing, Inc.
Cost:	$69
Hardware requirements:	Apple IIc or Enhanced IIe, with extended 80-column card and printer (*Pinpoint* will work with most dot matrix printers—e.g., Apple ImageWriter, Apple Scribe, Apple dot matrix, Epson RX series, MX, MX Grafrax+, Epson FX series, Okidata 92, and custom printer setup listed in program). Only these printers will work with *GraphMerge* (which puts pictures into word processing files): Apple ImageWriter series, Apple Scribe, and Apple dot matrix, C. Itoh ProWriter, and NEC 8023. Scribe or ImageWriter series must use Apple Super Serial card. Contact vendor to ascertain that proper printer is available. Only one disk drive is required, but two are preferable.
Description:	*Pinpoint* is combination software integrator, communications software, graphics system, calculator, and desk assistant, with automated appointment schedule, calendar, and notepad. Easy to install and use. Installation includes printer setup, modem setup, and other typical hardware. Some programs more useful than others. For instance, *Typewriter* is only marginally useful to most people (if at all); others are a dream (with Apple Writer), as are graphics and windows. Communications package has many useful features, including macros (automatic typing) for dialing your favorite networks or bulletin boards. *GraphMerge* inserts pictures, such as graphs, charts, or high-resolution graphics into word processing files, making otherwise routine reports come alive. Pictures may be altered by special widening or stretching commands, making them higher or wider, and by inverse command for entire illustration. Other accessories may be added (up to 16) from Pinpoint's library of programs. Exciting program, *Pinpoint* keeps Apple computer up to date with newest software.
Documentation:	Excellent 213-page manual, with screenshots, tutorial, five appendixes (printers, accessories, etc.), and index

Name:	**SideKick**
Program type:	Desktop accessory
Vendor:	Borland International, Inc.
Cost:	$84.95
Hardware requirements:	IBM PC, compatibles (25K)

Description: Neat program emulates many items we use on our desk every day: calendar/appointment book, notepad, calculator, dialer—and works very well indeed. Directory of phone numbers, with names and addresses, may be created for dialer for voice communications (sample directory comes with system); then center cursor line on name you want and dialing commences. Notepad is a word processor with unusual abilities: in addition to typing in your notes for future reference, the notepad will capture whatever is on the screen, whether a *WordStar* menu, batch of text, mass of numbers from spreadsheet—whatever; they can be saved and put into any other program. (There is no need to leave whatever program you are running to do this; just pause while your idea is saved to disk, whether you are using a spreadsheet or playing *Space Invaders*.) This is a particularly good feature for word processing, where charts or other material can be put into documents (in this sense, *SideKick* is an integrator; it makes a number of programs compatible). Appointment and calendar function appears to have no limit, with accommodations beyond the year 2000 (for people who truly plan ahead). Month-by-month calendar is shown on screen, and particular date is highlighted for appointment entry, 8 a.m. to 9 p.m. at half-hour intervals. Two other handy features are pop-up ASCII table and "import/export" data ability.

Documentation: 122-page manual of clear, concise instructions and examples

Word Processing

Introduction

Of all the uses to which a microcomputer may be put, word processing is undoubtedly the best. You can live without arcade games, without a fancy accounting package, and without a mouse, but you can't get along without a typewriter. In many ways, a word processing package can replace the typewriter, relegating it to a backup position. A microcomputer word processing system can so increase the efficiency and productivity of those who use it that one hears the term "technological cripple," referring to someone who finds it difficult or impossible to continue working if the plug is pulled on his or her monitor.

What, exactly, is a word processor, and what does it do? The marvels of the word processor are many. With such a computer program, it is possible to perform radical surgery on a document by "cut and paste"; i.e., to reformat, reedit, and reprint any document as often as required, without retyping more than needs to be changed or rearranged to create a new document from parts of others. Work is "saved out" to disk and retrieved whenever necessary—reworked in an infinite loop.

There are well over 100 programs for a microcomputer, including one (or more) for nearly every microcomputer made. They range in price from free to several hundred dollars, from systems which do little more than basic word processing to those which are "integrated" to work as part of a larger package, which often includes a spreadsheet and a database manager, and sometimes other programs for telecommunications.

Once programs are installed, text is sent to the buffer for temporary storage, saved to disk, retrieved, edited, and saved again—as often as required. Text may be printed out in many forms, and changed with a single command (e.g., from double- to triple-spaced, etc.).

It's true that "memory typewriters" or "dedicated word processors" do many of these things, but they are usually much more expensive, and they

119

never do more than run a single program. Since many libraries already own a microcomputer, an additional (and often inexpensive) software package is all they need for word processing capability. (And you can still play *Space Invaders* on the microcomputer when no one is looking!)

Add-Ons

Spelling, grammar, and word selection may be aided, too. "Spellers" don't ensure perfect spelling; they just help clear up typos. For instance, by running your document through a speller, the following errors can be corrected: *teh* (the), *assisttant,* or *villian.* Usually, a new word is substituted during the checking process, but suspect words may be marked for consideration. A frequently used word that is spelled correctly but is not in the standard spelling program (Jones or other proper nouns, for instance) may be added to the dictionary. A spelling program would *not* find an incorrectly used word, such as *through* for *threw* or *too* for *two.* So careful proofreading is always a good idea, no matter how good the spelling program.

Other program groups include the electronic thesaurus, grammar checker, and mailmerge. Instead of consulting a printed thesaurus, writers may simply ask the computer for a list of suitable words, from which a substitute may be chosen and automatically inserted. Many grammatical errors may also be found, as well as trite or overused phrases. These programs also improve one's writing, not just correct it. Writers will make the same mistakes less often, as they become aware of their errors. Mailmerge produces "personalized" letters from a name and address file.

Many libraries have been experimenting with microcomputer-based word processing. Of 200 libraries, according to my survey in late 1984, 60 (30%) were using a microcomputer in this fashion. The types of word processing varied considerably, from very basic programs, such as *Homeword* or *Bank Street Writer,* to very sophisticated programs, such as *WordStar.*

Word Processing in Libraries

Word processing is used in libraries for just about everything—from catalog card production to correspondence to paying bills and typing board minutes. The list includes

Agendas	Correspondence
Bibliographies	*dBase* programs
Board minutes	Department and system reports
Budget/accounting	Form letters

General administrative work	Printing of serial holdings
Grant applications	Reserve booklists
Librarian's monthly report	Speeches
Memos	Staff handbooks
Newsletter	Statistical reports
Personnel files	Videocassette holdings lists
Policies and procedures	

In short, just about anything that might be done with a typewriter, and more, may be done with a word processor—with greater efficiency.

Complex writing skills—requiring cut and paste, for example—are most dramatically assisted. For instance, although an annotated bibliography has been arranged alphabetically, a word processor easily rearranges the list by subject, or in other ways. (Specialized database management programs may be more efficient for some types of work [e.g., a bibliography], but also more expensive.) Tables may be inserted in a document wherever desired, monthly reports may be compiled into an annual report, and material in a table or other report may be shifted right or left, up or down.

Another handy feature is the creation of templates to distill many documents from one. Once a basic form has been developed, it may be used over and over, by changing the name, date, or other information.

However, there is much more to decision-making than software. Here are some essential components for good word processing:

Microcomputer	Software
Monitor	Word processing program
Printer	Spelling checker
Disk drives	Grammar checker
Internal RAM memory	Online thesaurus
80-column card	Mailmerge

Each component represents a big decision in itself, and the process can take months. Often, however, the hardware is already there, waiting (as it were) for someone to purchase a useful software package.

Hardware

The "hardware portion" of the survey reflects the many microcomputers in use by libraries:

Apple	20	(38%)
IBM	12	(22.6%)
TRS-80	6	(11.3%)

The weakest link in the word processing chain, however, is often the printer, and a great deal of attention should be given to what is the best type to buy (see the section "All about Printers," earlier in this volume).

With several hundred microcomputer word processing packages available, including integrated software, it is easy to see how popular word processing is—and how difficult the decision. So let us look at what libraries are using. The most popular package in libraries and among librarians according to survey results, was *WordStar* (22%), a CP/M program available for many microcomputers. Next in popularity was *AppleWriter* (16%), an Apple computer program. Table 1 shows the selected word processing systems in use on the corresponding microcomputers at the libraries surveyed.

Table 1: Survey Results Showing Use of Word Processing Systems and Microcomputers in Libraries

Word Processor	Microcomputer	In Use	Percentage
AppleWorks	Apple	1	1.6
AppleWriter	Apple II+/IIe	10	16.0
Bank Street Writer	Apple II+/IIe IBM PC	3	4.8
Framework	IBM PC	1	1.6
Homeword	Apple II+	1	1.6
MultiMate	TI Professional	2	3.2
Peachtext (CP/M)	Zenith 100	1	1.6
Perfect Writer	Kaypro II / 4/84 Columbia 1600-4	5	8.0
PFS:Write	IBM PC Apple IIe	6	9.6
Screenwriter	Apple IIe	3	4.8
Scripsit	TRS-80 II/III/16A	4	6.3
Superscripsit	TRS-80 III/IV	3	4.8
Volkswriter	IBM/Columbia MPC	1	1.6
WordStar (CP/M)	Various	14	22.0

Levels of Sophistication

The first thing to remember is that it is better to have *a* word processor than *no* word processor—there is no such thing as a *perfect* word processor. Choosing a word processor is a *personal* choice. The *best* selection should not be dictated by fashion or money (or lack thereof).

To look at every word processor carefully—to examine just a few—

would take months, but certain elements or criteria may help make a more objective, if not altogether speedy, decision.

For convenience, I have divided word processing programs into four groups or levels and reviewed packages which are representative of each level. The selection criteria (or features) are divided the same way: the more advanced (higher-level) word processors have more of these features than simpler systems. Obviously, there is always an overlap in any hierarchy, but the point is to introduce the reader to important differences. The levels are as follows.

Elementary. Line-oriented editors could be put into this category, but since such systems are not thought of as true word processors, they are not considered. Whereas a line editor allows users to edit only one line at a time, full-screen-oriented editors allow the user to go quickly from line to line and move, add, or delete text at any part of the document. Screen editors do this with varying sophistication. Simple screen-oriented systems, such as *Bankstreet Writer* and *Homeword,* permit the editing of an entire screen at one time.

These word processors do a better job than an electric typewriter, but have few (if any) advanced features, such as custom design of pages. All you get are the bare necessities.

Intermediate. This level includes many fine systems, such as *Apple-Writer*, *PFS:Write,* and *Magic Window.* They are adequate for all but the most advanced assignments. Such features as boilerplate, significant formatting, file manipulation, and advanced cursor control may be lacking.

Advanced. At this level are systems such as *WordStar, MacWrite,* and *SuperScripsit,* where little should be missing. They should have complete cursor control, file handling capability, and be able to customize the system to your needs. They should also have a compatible spelling program.

Integrated. At this level we find *Framework* and *AppleWorks,* and software families, such as *WordStar* and *PFS:Write,* also fall in this category. Not all integrated word processing systems are necessarily better than those described above, in lower categories, but they offer special advantages. The big plus is the ability to switch from word processor to spreadsheet or database management, or to integrate data or move them from one component to another (e.g., to incorporate charts or graphs into a document, easily and quickly). Not all integrated software are the same. A few are reviewed here, but others are discussed in the chapter "Integrated Software."

Features to Look For

1. *Cursor Control.* Does the program allow for quick, easy control of the cursor? I rank this as very important. At the bare

minimum, it should be possible to move the cursor in four directions, by one character and by more than one. It should also be possible to move the page up and down ("scroll").

2. *Live Screen.* A live screen means that changes (editing) may occur at the same time that text is entered. This cuts down tremendously on the time required to produce a document.

3. *File Manipulation.* Does the program have good file control? Check for boilerplate. That is, it should be possible to save to disk portions of a document or to append files both to files already on disk and to files already in the buffer. If the system is limited by the computer's RAM, it must be possible to chain files together. If not, the word processor is inferior.

4. *Backup Protection.* It should be possible to make a backup of the word processing program itself. If not, a backup copy should come with the program (i.e., 2 copies of the master program disk should be included in the package).

5. *Format Capability.* It should be easy to generate the final printed copy. In some programs, such as *WordStar,* "what you see is what you get." That is, the text is formatted as you edit. If the program does not generate "what you see," it should generate softcopy separately, which will save a great deal of time in the editing process.

6. *Support.* Is the vendor willing and able to answer questions over the phone? Is the documentation clear, and more important, does it cover everything? Is there a tutorial to help get you started? A reference card?

7. *Defaults.* Is it possible to change the printer slot or type, page dimensions, or slot and drive of the program? These capabilities allow customization of the program.

8. *Telecommunications.* This is optional, since many telecommunications packages do a much better job than word processing telecommunications options, which are often added on for sales promotion and not as serious tools.

9. *Speed.* How quickly can text be entered, moved from the editor to the formatter, and files be loaded and saved? Is it necessary to go through many clumsy help screens or menus? How fast does the screen scroll?

10. *Search Commands.* Be sure you have all the important commands, including search, search and replace, and global search and replace.

11. *Error Handling.* A good word processor should never "hang up" while editing, and some programs allow for "undoing" a routine after a mistake. Often, the delete function of text or files can easily destroy work and, as a result, some programs automatically make a backup copy of each text file. Decide what safety features you want.

12. *Add-Ons.* Is a spelling program available? Mailmerge? Thesaurus?

13. *Text Buffer and Copying Text.* Some word processors make it possible to copy a line or group of lines quickly; others do not.

14. *Wordwrap.* Nearly all word processors now have wordwrap: when the cursor reaches the end of a line, the last word is "wrapped," or moved to the beginning of the next line, obviating the need to hit the "return" key or carriage return. This is an important advance over the typewriter.

15. *Deleting Text.* It should be possible to key a character, line, or block into oblivion, instantly.

16. Here's a checklist of other features to consider for efficient word processing: right justification, centering, margin control, headers, footers, automatic pagination, double and triple spacing, sub- and superscript, boldface, italic, underlining, split-screen editing, macros, index creation, and table of contents creation.

Sources of Additional Information

Block, David, and Aydan Kalyoncu. "Selection of Word Processing Software for Library Use," *Information Technology and Libraries,* September 1983, p. 253.

Consumer Guide. *Easy-to-Understand Guide to Word Processing.* Beekman House, 1984, 95 pp. $3.98.

Good, Phillip I. *Choosing a Word Processor.* Reston, 1982, 193 pp. $12.95.

Hutchinson, Warner A., and Betty Hutchinson. *Word Processing Made Simple.* Doubleday, 1984, 128 pp. $4.95.

Johnson, Kate Lee. *The Apple Writer II Handbook for the IIe.* Van Nostrand, 1984, 198 pp. $19.50.

Justie, Kevin M. "Word Processing Software: Applications," *Apple Library User's Group Newsletter,* October 1985, p. 42.

McWilliams, Peter. *The Word Processing Book: A Short Course in Computer Literacy.* Prelude Press, 1982, 270 pp. $9.95.

Moskowitz, Mickey. "Use an Apple to Save a Tree: Word Processing with the Microcomputer," *Technicalities,* January 1, 1983, p. 11.

Naiman, Arthur. *Word Processing Buyer's Guide.* McGraw-Hill, 1983, 325 pp. $15.95.

Sommer, Elyse. *Perfect Writer Made Perfectly Clear.* Chilton, 1984, 171 pp. $12.95.

Stern, Fred. *Word Processing and Beyond.* Muir, 1983, 221 pp. $9.95.

Reviews

Apple Writer II

Bank Street Writer II

Grammatik II

Homeword

Homeword Speller

MacWrite 4.5

Perfect Writer

PFS:Write

Scripsit/SuperScripsit

Sensible Grammar

Sensible Speller IV

Word Finder

WordPerfect

WordStar

Name:	**Apple Writer II**
Program type:	Word processing
Vendor:	Apple Computer, Inc.
Hardware requirements:	Apple IIe, IIc
Price:	$89
Used at:	Southwest State Texas University Learning Resources Center J. C. Kellam Building, Room 401 San Marcos, TX 78666 512-245-2286
Description:	*Apple Writer* may be purchased as individual package or as part of *AppleWorks,* an integrated software package, though latter is less powerful and has fewer features than standalone program, which in many ways is excellent.

Glossary features allow user to create "macro," or library of lengthy or difficult-to-type terms which become one-letter substitutions in text. For instance, instead of "Universal Software Package International Brotherhood," "*" might be typed. Phrase is automatically inserted by word processor from glossary file. Global search and replace commands of many word processors do the same, but not as conveniently.

Allows wide variety of changes in print, including left or right justification of text, or both. Also has global search and replace. All DOS commands accessible from single menu within *Apple Writer*. Page formatting is simple, too; online menu contains all settings for formatted page and serves as memory prompt. Other outstanding feature is *Apple Writer's* split-screen function for comparing two parts of a document in memory. Also allows transfer of text from one window to other, so that document of frequently used phrases or paragraphs ("boilerplate") can be created and drawn upon as needed, saving much retyping. Good selection of help menus is great advantage for novice.

Additional
information: "Producing Information Cards for the Card Catalog Using *Apple Writer II," Apple Library User's Group Newsletter,* January 1985, p. 37.

Name: **Bank Street Writer II**

Program type: Word processing

Vendor: Broderbund Software, Inc.

Cost: $69.95 (Apple), $79.95 (IBM PC)

Hardware
requirements: Apple II series (80-column display only with IIe and c); IBM PC, XT, PCjr.

Used at: Harvey W. Scott Library
Pacific University
Forest Grove, OR 97116
503-351-6151 ext. 231

Description: The ultimate in simplicity and friendliness, and can be in use 15 minutes after receipt. Capacity for normal Apple II+ is 1300 words, or 3200 words if used with 64K. Major drawback, if used with II+, is placement of key for uppercase (∧), which makes for awkward typing and slows the process considerably. Still, program has much to recommend it, especially if used for public access or simple library chores.

Menu-driven. To move, replace, erase, transfer, or retrieve text, menu routine is necessary, which also slows writing process. Other problems are limited cursor control (4 direction keys: up or down 12 lines and to beginning or end of text); no control over formatting (program is preformatted—and that's that). Not a full-feature word processing package.

Documentation: Slender but sufficient booklet and online tutorial

Related
programs: *Activities for Bank Street Writer, Bank Street Filer, Bank Street Mailer, Bank Street Speller*

Name: **Grammatik II**

Program type: Grammar checker

Vendor: Reference Software, Inc.

Cost: $89

Hardware
requirements: IBM PC

Description: *Grammatik* has been around some time, and *Grammatik II* is new, improved version. However, beta test copy was supplied for this review, so our judgments may not be final (query your vendor on finished product). That said, it seems to be an amazing program, a writer's dream. *Grammatik* is not a word processing program in itself, but a supplement. For example, it will take a file prepared by *WordStar* and search for errors. It helps writers avoid many pitfalls in archaic usage, capitalization, punctuation, pretentious usage, coinage, trite phrases, vague adverbs, split infinitives, wordy passages, etc.

Grammatik comes with large internal phrase dictionary, but may be customized by user to recognize other mistakes. System is configured in a few minutes. The main program file or phrase dictionary contains 600 phrases, and operation is similar to *Sensible Speller* and *Sensible Grammar* (and other spelling programs in this volume). Program scans document file, then highlights each suspicious phrase, allowing options of ignoring it, marking it for consideration, or—if marked or changed file is not used—creating backup file of the original, untouched document.

Example: Program, upon checking a document, finds "a number of," which it declares to be "wordy." "Suggestion" is to use "most," "many," "several," "some," or "few."

Following this, additional information (on summary screen) includes readability, word and sentence statistics, and so on. Then file is compared to three written works: Gettysburg Address, Hemingway short story, and life insurance policy. Depending upon how much detail the user requires, grammar and punctuation errors may be marked with only a "#" sign or ignored. Exciting program for anyone concerned about finished products. Neither this nor any program will find all mistakes or errors, but all programs make user aware of many common problems.

Documentation:	All necessary information contained in extensive documentation. List of error messages, as well as directions on how to customize program with your phrases, is included, plus step-by-step walkthrough instructions.
Name:	**Homeword**
Program type:	Word processor
Vendor:	Sierra On-Line, Inc.
Cost:	$69, Apple II series, Commodore 64; $75, IBM PC, PCjr.
Hardware requirements:	Apple II series, Commodore 64, IBM PC, PCjr.
Description:	This popular word processing program (for home use) was designed for young and older students and adults with marginal writing needs. Nevertheless, some libraries have found it adequate, and it is excellent public access program since it requires virtually no time to learn (which makes *Homeword* so popular). Menu of "icons" (tiny drawings across bottom of screen) represents major modes of operation (e.g., a printer for printing, file cabinet for saving or loading from disk); similar in this respect (though more modest) to Apple Macintosh icons. Users need memorize few (if any) commands,

relying instead upon visual display. Merely position icon cursor over desired function, then hit return key.

Useful work can be accomplished after a single session; there are problems, however. Icons don't, in all cases, look like what they represent, but more like a tangle of arrows pointing in all directions. Fortunately, the *meaning* of each drawing is printed beneath it. Program limitations are awkward keystroke combinations for cursor control and need to exit edit mode to copy or move blocks of text. Other features associated with professional-quality word processor are lacking. For instance, it is impossible to delete entire word or phrase in one operation; anything shorter than entire line must be deleted one letter at a time.

Though I managed to create and print a file from screen to printer in less than half an hour (and in 80-column mode through high-resolution graphics), scroll was painfully slow. Still, because some people will not spend the time to learn more powerful system, this simple word processor is several steps above their typewriter. For public access, there is nothing better.

Documentation:	Written documentation is so simple that it is skimpy, even though audiocassette of instructions is supplied.

Name:	**Homeword Speller**
Program type:	Spelling correction
Vendor:	Sierra On-line, Inc.
Cost:	$49.95 (Can be purchased as complete package, with *Homeword Writer* and *Homeword Filer,* for $149.95)
Description:	*Homeword Speller* is similar in operation and strength to *Sensible Speller,* but there are differences. *Homeword Speller* is a good menu-driven program and, like *Homeword* itself, its main menu is five-line series of drawings or icons, each representing a function. Selection menu includes Edit Wordbook, File, Check Spelling, Customize, and Disk Utilities.

Homeword Speller operates more slowly than *Sensible Speller* (reviewed below) and its dictionary is not as impressive (only 28,000 words); however, users may add 5000 words or compile their own dictionaries. Nor does *Homeword Speller* return as much information to users as *Sensible Speller*. Recommended to *Homeword* owners primarily for public access, for which it is ideal, being easy to use. Program is compatible with most ASCII files.

Documentation: Very good booklet, reference card, and audiotape provide comprehensive instructions.

Name: **MacWrite 4.5**

Program type: Word processor

Vendor: Apple Computer, Inc.

Cost: Free (bundled with Macintosh)

Hardware
requirements: Macintosh, Imagewriter, or Laserwriter

Description: More often than not, users are too satisfied with their new Macintosh to appraise a Mac program accurately ("It's as good as anything gets!"). Although they have much to be happy about, there *are* problems, especially with the *MacWrite* word processing program—though it can be recommended for several reasons.

A "what you see is what you get" system, *MacWrite* allows selection among many fonts with the click of a mouse. Search and replace features are limited, however, in that *MacWrite* will only search forward. The two best features of *MacWrite* (in fact, of the Macintosh) are its pull-down windows and mouse (a small, hand-held box connected to the computer by a cord). When the mouse is moved on a flat surface, there is a corresponding cursor movement on the screen. This obviates the need to learn much about cursor control commands and reduces keyboard interaction.

However, most experienced writers, and especially computer users, find learning to use the mouse is like plowing through *Homeword*'s icon list: time consuming. The mouse does *not* reduce the rate of error because less typing is required to print or otherwise handle documents; it is just as easy to make an error *with* the mouse. People who must generate vast amounts of text don't want to be hampered, and won't abandon their "traditional" program. There is also the need for extra mouse desk space, and moving one's hands back and forth across the desk, from keyboard to mouse, dilutes concentration.

MacPaint is the graphics package that comes with the Macintosh. The two programs are integrated, and graphics or information can be put in the "Scrapbook" for use with any other Mac application. Major advantage is that they permit creation and placement of top-quality graphics in any document. Almost uniquely, *MacWrite* makes many elaborate operations possible. For instance, if you want a fancy font, just press a key and the whole text will look as if it was prepared by a calligrapher. But without a good dot matrix printer, this capability is worthless, as is the ability to integrate *MacPaint,* since graphics do not show up on daisywheel printers. If your most urgent word processing need is to generate text, you will probably want to use another program.

Other pluses for *MacWrite* include the many advantages of the Macintosh. The Mac sits comfortably on a desk, where space is at a premium, and is rather attractive. Disk storage for the Mac is formidable, about 320K. Hard disk storage, available from various manufacturers, comes with its built-in accessories of notepad, calculator, alarm clock, and even puzzles for amusement during an idle moment.

Additional information:	Anderson, Eric. "The Library Macintosh: A Special Report for the Apple Library User's Group," *Apple Library User's Group Newsletter,* October 1985, p. 26. A comprehensive examination of Macintosh microcomputer in a library.
Related software:	*Art à la Mac* (2 vols.). Springboard. $39.95 each. Provides 1200 pieces of clip art for *MacWrite* and *MacPaint.*
Name:	**Perfect Writer**
Program type:	Word processor

Vendor: Thorn EMI Computer Software

Cost: $199, IBM PC (128K)
$139, Apple

Hardware
requirements: IBM PC, XT, Apple IIe, IIc (128K)

Used at: ABC-Clio Library
Box 4397
Santa Barbara, CA 93103
805-963-4221
(Hope Smith Special Library)

Description: *Perfect Writer,* part of software family that includes exceptional spreadsheet, and a spelling program, *Perfect Speller,* which has 50,000-word expandable dictionary. Thesaurus of 50,000 synonyms helps writers find the right word. *Perfect Writer* also has excellent cursor control, split-screen editing, and default or custom formatting. Another advanced feature is ability to create alphabetical index of selected words at end of a manuscript, with page references. Also provides automatic footnote positioning and formatting on proper page, headings (numbered and unnumbered), footers, typeface commands, and page numbers. Using headings, *Perfect Writer* will also produce table of contents with page numbers. Up to seven documents may be stored in memory at once.

Documentation: Manual details all important features, start-up instructions, and general operation.

Related
programs: *Perfect Calc* ($249)

Additional
information: Sommer, Elyse. *Perfect Writer Made Perfectly Clear.* Chilton, 1984.

Name: **PFS:Write**

Program type: Word processing

Vendor: Software Publishing Corporation
Scholastic Version

Cost: $115

Hardware
requirements: Apple II series; IBM PC; XT; compatibles

Description: *PFS:Write* comes in several versions, including one for teachers, which is what we were sent upon request. This excellent product, which makes word processing easy and fun, is most impressive because of its lack of extended start-up or learning period. Most people can grasp the fundamentals almost instantly, documentation is adequate (even a handy card for quick reference). Commands are much the same as for other PFS modules. Ctrl-C is used to continue, instead of "return" key, which makes it difficult to err unintentionally. Cursor control permits "goto," line #, beginning and end of document. I could not, however, find a "home" key (which moves cursor from top to bottom, or conversely). Text must be highlighted in order to duplicate.

Main menu has five options: type/edit, define page, print, get/save/remove, and clear. Important to note that setting up page or print options is very easy and allows for menu-driven definition of four margins, page length, heading, and footing. Print option screen includes from and to page print, pause between pages (yes or no), indent, insertion of *PFS:Graphs* or *Files* into document, and help option.

This Scholastic edition has disk of sample documents, including Asimov's essay "Three Laws of Robotics" (among other things), supplied for practice. Overall, a good writing instrument for most library work.

Documentation: Excellent manual gives clear directions and instructions (with screenshots) for each section of *PFS:Write*. Also a section on learning activities for classroom.

Related
programs: PFS has its own spelling checker, *PFS:Proof* ($95).

Name: **Scripsit/SuperScripsit**

Program type: Word processor

Vendor: Radio Shack

Cost: Prices vary considerably, depending on version

Hardware
requirements: TRS-80 Model III

Description: This Radio Shack system has a number of good
              features—once confusion between *Scripsit* and *Super-Scripsit* is removed. Latter did not replace the former;
              both are available. *SuperScripsit,* however, is more
              sophisticated—a better "what you see is what you get"
              format. Most versions of *Scripsit* use printer codes
              which must be embedded in text. If word processor is
              needed for a TRS-80, this one should be seriously
              considered.

Name: **Sensible Grammar**

Program type: Document proofreader

Vendor: Sensible Software, Inc.

Cost: $99.95

Hardware
requirements: Apple II series, 128K; ProDOS. (Comes on 5½-inch
              floppy and 3½-inch disks [you can return the one not
              needed for a backup of the other]. Program will work on
              hard disk drive or only one floppy.)

Description: Splendid package corrects many simple but overlooked
              grammatical errors. Not a word processor, but intended
              for use with files created by word processing programs.
              Setup is simple; it is preprogrammed for a number of
              word processors. Just select correct procedure from
              setup menu. Program uses "pop-up" windows of
              ProDOS, and operates much the same way as *Sensible
              Speller* (reviewed below), displaying offending or sus-
              pect phrase (e.g., "exhibit a tendency to") and giving
              users option to (I)gnore, (R)eplace, (M)ark, (E)nter, or
              (P)rint it. Over 1000 phrases in dictionary. Considerable
              flexibility allowed in selecting phrases, and user may ac-
              tivate only certain categories: clichés, contractions,
              legal terms, and faulty, informal, personal, redundant,
              sexist, vague, or wordy phrases. Very much like a per-
              sonal tutor, since users learn as they work, making

subsequent documents more acceptable as errors are avoided. Also, there is no embarrassment, as when one human (however well intentioned) edits another.

Sensible Grammar may be transferred to work on most ProDOS-compatible hard disk drives, using utilities package. Works with most ProDOS word processors available for Apple II series, including *Apple-Works, Apple Writer, Format II, Mouse Write, PFS:Write, Word Juggler,* and *Zardax.*

Documentation: Eighty-eight–page looseleaf binder. Extensive setup instructions answer most installation questions. Manual is excellent reference guide, describing operation, error handling, utilities, and much more in easy-to-follow format. Index.

Name: **Sensible Speller IV**

Program type: Spelling program

Vendor: Sensible Software, Inc.

Cost: $125

Hardware
requirements: Apple II, II+, IIe; one or two disk drives; 48K

Additional
information: "The Sensible Speller" (review), *Nibble Magazine,* April 1984, p. 65.

Related
programs: Works with most Apple DOS word processing systems, including *WordStar, Apple Writer,* and most CP/M word processing systems. Two special versions are also available, one for Apple Pascal and one for Apple ProDOS. *Sensible Speller* does *not* work with *Cut & Paste, Easy Writer,* or *Incredible Jack.* Also, does not permit advanced functions (specifically, access to thesaurus or immediate spelling correction) if used in CP/M, Pascal, *PFS:Write,* or *Word Handler* forms.

Description: Easy to use and flexible, with ability to increase dictionary size, change drives or slot numbers, utilize upper- and lowercase, etc. Getting started takes a few seconds or up to 20 minutes, depending on customization. Unlike earlier programs, spelling errors can be corrected within program (whereas other spellers requried that errors be "marked" with user-selected symbol, and corrected later with word processing program, thereby wasting valuable time). Words may be added to dictionary at the same time.

Adding words is relatively simple and may be done several ways. Word documents may be added wholesale—though this is usually not practical, unless document is word collection processed specifically for this purpose. Best and simplest way is to add words as documents are checked (though not permitted in every version of this program). Dictionary that comes with system is quite general and contains 80,000 words. Fortunately, these words are not constructed from roots, but are the actual words themselves. By adding frequently used words (e.g., *Dewey Decimal System,* names of correspondents, or other proper nouns), it is possible to further reduce time needed to check a document. Approximately 10,000 words may be added to system dictionary, but as many custom dictionaries as required may be created on separate disks.

Speller main menu allows "utilities" or "check a document." If latter is chosen, program will ask that document disk be inserted into disk drive, then collect document's words. Document disk is replaced by dictionary disk in disk drive, and program compares dictionary words with document words. User may then check the document against another dictionary. (Main dictionary [about 40,000 words] resides on front of dictionary disk; supplementary dictionary [about 40,000 less commonly used words] resides on back. Customized dictionaries may be stored separately on other disks.) Once complete, remaining suspect words (which could not be identified in one of the dictionaries) may be viewed or printed out. As each word is viewed on screen (have a print dictionary handy), several one-letter options are available: (I)gnore the word, (M)ark the word, (G)uess at correct spelling (from program's dictionary), (R)eplace the word (with your correct spelling), and (A)dd the word to dictionary.

When finished, document disk is returned to drive and document changes are made automatically (since program creates a work file, there must be equal blank space on floppy disk or spelling program will "abort," making it necessary to start over). If correct spelling is guessed, program will list words in *Random House Dictionary* that are close to misspelled word. Sometimes this helps, sometimes not. it is usually much better to "look up" the word in a dictionary. Program is not a grammar checker, so if a word is not used in its proper context, or *two* is used instead of *too,* the software has no way of knowing; so careful proofreading should not be abandoned. This and other spelling programs can reduce the number of typos and spelling goofs to which many are prone.

Documentation: Looseleaf notebook of instructions and hints is excellent and has over 100 pages and four appendixes ("Taking Care of Problems," "How to Set Up for Specific Word processors," "Hardware Setup" and "Entering Special Symbols.") Index.

Related
Products: Several supplemental, specialized dictionaries are available, such as 20,000-word *Black's Law Dictionary* and *Stedman's Medical Dictionary* ($99.95 each).

Name: **Word Finder**

Program type: Electronic thesaurus

Vendor: Writing Consultants

Cost: $124.95

Hardware
requirements: IBM PC and compatibles (takes 35K of RAM space)

Description: *Word Finder* is electronic equivalent of *Roget's Thesaurus*, with 9000 key words and 90,000 synonyms. Most people are now familiar with spelling programs, but not with other writing aids. So first thought is: "Is this an improvement over the printed thesaurus I already use?" I decided to keep my copy for the time being, but found at least one advantage in the new method: speed. Users no longer must turn through pages of text, looking for a synonym; words now appear electronically, on a screen from within the word processor. For thoroughness, I find that my book offers better, in-depth analysis of relationships between words, categories, and parts of speech (noun, adjective, etc.). But the computerized version excels in quick changes, operated from the keyboard.

Word Finder can be up and running in about five mintues, and may be operated from within or outside the word processing program. After *Word Finder* is loaded, it can be summoned by a two-key sequence. There's no trick to making it work. The word upon which the cursor lay when the thesaurus was called is the word with which the program works. A list of synonyms is displayed on the bottom half of the screen and the user quickly and easily substitutes any word—or none—with a keystroke.

Program may also be used *without* a word processor, though the word-replacement feature will not work perfectly. The new version of the program may be reconfigured if a different word processor is used (originally, the "install" program would run once— period). *Word Finder* can be used with several word processing programs for the IBM PC, including *ReallyStar, WordStar 2000, Multimate, WordPerfect, Writing Assistant, PFS:Write, Microsoft,* and *Easy Writer II;* and there is a "generic" form.

Documentation: Twelve-page booklet completely explains the system.

Name: **WordPerfect**

Program type: Word processor

Vendor: WordPerfect Corporation

Cost: $495

Hardware
requirements: IBM PC, AT, XT; 256K

Description: *WordPerfect* has many advanced features, such as math and macro functions, table of contents, indexes, outlines, and more. Also, it is easy to use, especially when compared with other word processors in its class, such as *WordStar*. An interesting feature is the program's ability to handle columns of text. When it produces two columns on a page for a newsletter, for example, each column may be edited separately, without difficulty — something many word processors cannot do. It, too, is a "what you see is what you get" word processor, including the column handling.

Its good features seem endless. Mailmerge is included, as is a "type through" feature which lets the computer be used like a typewriter. It also supports a split screen and an "undo" feature. (It is difficult to imagine what may have been left out.) Improvements over earlier versions of *WordPerfect* include a built-in spelling checker and thesaurus. (The dictionary for the spelling checker has about 115,000 words.) If a library needs a top-of-the-line word processor, this is the best one currently available. There is also a learning disk or tutorial.

Documentation:	Two excellent manuals, one for installation and one with illustrations and screenshots, help users get started almost immediately.
Additional information:	"WordPerfect 4.1: The Best Improved," *InfoWorld*, November 4, 1985, p. 41

Name:	**WordStar 3.3, WordStar 2000**
Program type:	Word processor
Vendor:	MicroPro International Corp.
Cost:	Varies considerably, depending on microcomputer, *WordStar* version, and discount by vendor. Also comes bundled with various microcomputers.
Hardware requirements:	Most CP/M-based microcomputers, and printer (either dot-matrix or daisywheel)
Description:	*WordStar* has long been considered the most sophisticated word processing package available for microcom-

puters. It has full features, and is part of an integrated system which offers many add-on packages. Also, it is usable by a wide variety of microcomputers, since it is CP/M-based. The spelling program *SpellStar* and the *MailMerge* package, as well as *Word Finder* (Writing Consultants), may be operated from within the program. *Sensible Speller* (for Apple computers only) is also compatible.

WordStar supports a host of additional features, such as proportional spacing, super- and subscript, and footnotes (if additional module is purchased and printer has such capability). *WordStar* probably has more "extras," provided by peripheral vendors, than any other word processing system (though many must be purchased separately).

Another important feature is "what you see is what you get." That is, the text is formatted on the screen *while* you work. This is important since many excellent microcomputer-based word processor programs will not format text on the screen, or require an extra step to do so. For most people this is not a problem. However, there are several real and important obstacles to consider.

The system is very difficult to master, and despite its many help screens it is confusing and awkward. Triple keystrokes for changing modes or functions make the program difficult to learn and very slow to operate. Although *WordStar* now comes in two versions (standard and *WordStar 2000*), configuring the system shows how hostile it can be. *WordStar* does *not* self-configure. Configuration menus seem to go on forever and make no sense to the average computer user, especially the novice, unless close attention is paid to the lengthy installation documentation. One writer has said about configuring *WordStar:* "Unless you are well versed in computers, it is almost impossible for you to initialize or install the program by yourself. . . . Insist on [help] from your dealer, before attempting to initialize your own program. It might save hours of agonizing futility." I don't agree it's *that* hard, but it is certainly not simple.

However, it can be configured for just about any type of hardware, being the ultimate in flexibility.

Documentation: *WordStar* comes with a manual of hundreds of pages, and separate sections cover installation, training, and reference. Instruction courses are popular and widely available.

Related
programs: *WordStar,* an integrated system, is compatible with a number of excellent add-on programs.

Infostar is a powerful, easy-to-use database management system.

CalcStar, an electronic spreadsheet, is similar to *VisiCalc* and other such systems. Finished products may be included in a *WordStar* manuscript.

Appendix A
A Directory of Library User Groups

Apple Library Users Group. Apple Computer (Monica Ertel), Corporate Documentation MS 26B, 20650 Valley Green Dr., Cupertino, Calif. 95014.

Appleworks User Group (Jim Willis), 1300 Hinton St., West Monroe, Ia. 71291.

Central Illinois Libraries Microcomputer User's Group (for libraries of all types). Parlin-Ingersoll Library (Randy Wilson), 205 W. Chestnut St., Canton, Ill. 61520.

Columbia User's Group (Philadelphia, Pa.) (includes community college and public libraries). (Jack A. Newcombe, Asst. Chief, Extension Division), Free Library of Philadelphia, 19th and Vine Sts., Philadelphia, Pa. 19103.

DTI (Data Trek, Inc.) User's Group (Northern California) (Kathy Westsik, Senior Information Specialist), Syntext Corp. Library, 3401 Hillview Ave., Palo Alto, Calif. 94304.

Illinois Heartland User's Group (IHUG) (Brenda Stenger, Reference Librarian), Illinois Farm Bureau, 1701 Towanda Ave., Bloomington, Ill. 61701.

Library User's Group—Zenith (LUGZ) (meetings every two months, membership $10 per year), Kansas State Library, State Capitol, Third Floor, Topeka, Kan. 66612.

Manitoba Online User's Group (K. Eric Marshall, Covenor), c/o Freshwater Institute, 501 University Crescent, Winnipeg, Manitoba, Canada R3T 2N6.

Microcomputer User Group for Libraries in North Carolina (MUGLNC) (membership $5 per year), Campbell University Law Library (Doris Hinson), Box 458, Buies Creek, N.C. 27506.

The Midwest CLSI User's Group (membership $15), Grand Rapids Public Library, (Martha Seaman, Technical Services), Grand Rapids Public Library, Library Plaza, Grand Rapids, Mich. 49503.

New England Microcomputer User's Group (annual dues $15), Graduate School of Library & Information Science (Ching-chih Chen), Simmons College, 300 The Fenway, Boston, Mass. 02115.

NOLA Regional Library System Microcomputer User Group, NOLA Regional Library System (Thresa A. Trucksis), 25 E. Boardman St., Youngstown, Ohio 44503.

Public Librarians Using Microcomputers (N.J.), Library Development Bureau (Marilyn Veldof, Consultant), New Jersey State Library, 185 W. State St. CN520, Trenton, N.J. 08625.

Rochester Regional Research Library Council Microcomputer User's Group, Rochester Regional Research Council (Kathleen Miller), 339 East Ave., Rm. 300, Rochester, N.Y. 14604.

Tennessee Library Association Microcomputer Roundtable, Hiwassee College, (Kent Millwood, President, Director of Library Services), Rt. 1, Madisonville, Tenn. 37354.

Upper Hudson Library Federation Apple User's Group (N.Y.), Troy Public Library, (Ruth A. Eveland, Director), 100 2nd St., Troy, N.Y. 12180.

Appendix B
Vendor List

Addison-Wesley Publishing Co., Jacobs Way, Reading, Mass. 01867.

Advanced Logic Systems, 1195 E. Arques Ave., Sunnyvale, Calif. 94086. 408-730-0307.

Androm Associates, Box 506, New Town Branch, Boston, Mass. 02258.

Apple Computer, Inc., 20525 Mariani Ave., Cupertino, Calif. 95014.

Ashton-Tate, 10150 W. Jefferson Blvd., Culver City, Calif. 90230.

Baudville, 1001 Medical Park Dr., S.E., Grand Rapids, Mich. 49506. 616-957-3036.

Beagle Bros. Micro Software, Inc., 3990 Old Town Ave., San Diego, Calif. 92110. 800-227-3800, ext. 1607.

Bill Blue, Marilla Corp., 1274 Del Monte Dr., El Cajon, Calif. 92020.

Borland International Inc., 4585 Scotts Valley Dr., Scotts Valley, Calif. 95066.

Broderbund Software, Inc., 17 Paul Dr., San Rafael, Calif. 94903. 415-479-1170.

Calico, Box 15916, St. Louis, Mo. 63114.

Cdex Intelligence Corporation, 1885 Lundy Ave., San Jose, Calif. 95131 408-263-0430 or 800-982-1213.

Center for the Study of Rural Librarianship, College of Library Science, Clarion University of Pennsylvania, Clairon, Pa. 16214.

Central Point Software, Inc., 9700 S.W. Capitol Highway, Portland, Ore. 97219.

Combase, Inc., Suite 890, 333 Sibley St., St. Paul, Minn. 55101.

Diversified Software Research, Inc., 5848 Crampton Ct., Rockford, Ill. 61111. 800-835-2246, ext. 127.

EasyNet, 9 Carleton Rd., Belmont, Mass. 02178. 617-484-2361.

Electronic Bookshelf, RR 9, Box 64, Frankfort, Ind. 46041. 317-324-2182.

ERIC Clearinghouse on Information Resources, 030 Huntington Hall, Syracuse University, Syracuse, N.Y. 13210.

ETT Library Automations, Inc., 9201 Drake Ave., Suite 103, Evanston, Ill. 60203. 312-677-7704.

Follett Software Co., 4506 Northwest Highway, Crystal Lake, Ill. 60014. 800-435-6170; in Illinois, 815-455-1100.

General Research Corp., Library Systems, Box 6770, Santa Barbara, Calif. 96160. 800-235-6788 or 805-964-7724.

Hayden Book Co., 50 E. Essex St., Roc Welle Park, Mass. 07662.

Hayes Microcomputer Products, Inc., 5923 Peachtree Industrial Blvd., Norcross, Calif. 30092. 404-449-8791.

Hi Willow Research and Publishing Co., Box 1801, Fayetteville, Ar. 72702.

Informatics General Corp., 6011 Executive Blvd., Rockville, Md. 20852. 301-770-3000 or 800-638-6595.

Information Access Co., 11 Davis Dr., Belmont, Calif. 94002. 800-227-8431.

Information/Documentation, Inc., Box 17109, Dulles Intl. Airport, Washington, D.C. 20041. 703-979-5363 or 800-336-5363.

Information Intelligence, Inc., Box 31098, Phoenix, Ariz. 85046. 602-996-2283.

InMagic, Inc., 238 Broadway, Cambridge, Mass. 02139. 617-661-8124.

K–12 MicroMedia Publishing, 172 Broadway, Dept. T, Woodcliff Lake, N.J. 07675. 800-922-0401; in New Jersey, 201-391-7555.

The Library Corporation, Box 40035, Washington, D.C. 20016. 800-624-0559.

Lotus Development Corp., 55 Cambridge Parkway, Cambridge, Mass. 02142.

McNeal Memorial Hospital, Health Sciences Resource Center, 3249 S. Oak Park Ave., Berwyn, Ill. 60402. 312-795-9100.

Media Center Factory, Box 13536, Greensboro, N.C. 27405.

Micro Data Products, Inc., 5739 S. Olathe Court, Aurora, Colo. 80015.

Micro Libraries (Eric Anderson), 20 Congress Ave., Sioux City, Ia. 51104.

Micro Power & Light Co., 12820 Hillcrest Rd., Dallas, Tex. 75230.

Microdex, Box 238, Battle Ground, Ind. 47920.

MicroPro International Corp., 33 San Pablo Ave., San Rafael, Calif. 94903. 415-499-1200.

Microsoft Corporation, 10700 Northup Way, Bellevue, Wash. 98004.

Micro-Systems Software, Inc., 1401–18 Oak Circle, Boca Raton, Fla. 33431. 305-391-5077.

Midwest Automated Technical Services System (MATSS), Director of Library Automation, 11443 St. Charles Rock Rd., Bridgeton, Md. 63004.

Mindscape, Inc., 3444 Dundee Rd., Northbrook, Ill. 60062.

MECC, 3490 Lexington Avenue N., St. Paul, Minn. 55126. 612-481-3500.

Personal Bibliograpic Software, Inc., Box 4250, Ann Arbor, Mich. 48106. 313-996-1580.

Pinpoint Publishing, Inc., Box 13323, Oakland, Calif. 95661. 415-530-1726.

Professional Software, 21 Forest Ave., Glen Ridge, N.J. 07028. 201-748-7658.

Quaid Software Limited, 620 Jarvis St., Suite 2412, Toronto, Ontario, Canada M4Y 2R8. 416-961-8243.

Radio Shack. Consult local dealer.

Reference Press, Box 1141, Station F, Toronto, Ontario, Canada M4Y 2T8. 416-960-3235.

Reference Software, Inc., 330 Townsend, Suite 232, San Francisco, Calif. 94107. 415-563-6322.

Richmond Software Corporation, 1650 Amphlett Blvd., Suite 205, San Mateo, Calif. 94402. 800-222-6063; in California, 415-349-6063.

Right On Programs, Box 977, Huntington, N.Y. 11743. 516-271-3177.

Rolodex Corp., 245 Secaucus Rd., Secaucus, N.J. 07094. 201-348-3939.

Scarecrow Press, Inc., 52 Liberty St., Metuchen, N.J. 08840.

Scholastic Software, Inc., 730 Broadway, New York, N.Y. 10003. 212-505-3000.

Sensible Software, Inc., 210 S. Woodward, Suite 229, Birmingham, Mich. 48011.

Sierra On-Line, Inc., Box 485, Coarsegold, Calif. 93614.

Silicon Valley Systems, Inc., 1625 El Camino Real, Belmont, Calif. 94002. 415-593-4344.

Small Library Computing, Inc., 48 Lawrence Ave., Holbrook, N.Y. 11741. 516-588-1387.

Society for Visual Education, Inc., 1345 Diversey Parkway, Chicago, Ill. 60614.

Software Publishing Corp., 1901 Landings Dr., Mountain View, Calif. 94043.

Sorcim Corporation, 2310 Lundy Ave., San Jose, Calif. 95131.

Southwestern Oregon Community College, Coos Bay, Ore. 97420.

Speak Softly, Inc., 303 Calvert Ave., Clingon, S.C. 29325.

Spectral Graphics Software, 6333 Pacific Ave., Suite 256, Stockton, Calif. 95207. 800-826-2989; in California, 800-231-7316.

Spectrum HoloByte, Inc., 1050 Walnut, Suite 325, Boulder, Colo. 80302.

Springboard Software, Inc., 7807 Creekridge Circle, Minneapolis, Minn. 55435. 612-944-3912.

Stoneware, Inc., 50 Belvedere St., San Rafael, Calif. 94901. 415-457-1656.

Swan Software, Box 206, Lititz, Pa. 17543. 717-627-1911.

Thorn EMI Computer Software, Inc., 285 Mill Rd., Chelmsford, Mass. 01824. 617-256-3900.

Unison World, 2150 Shattuck Ave., #902, Berkeley, Calif. 94704. 415-848-6666.

United Software Industries, 8399 Topanga Canyon Blvd., Suite 200, Canooce Park, Calif 91304. 818-887-5800.

Utilico Microware, 3377 Solano Ave., Suite 352, Napa, Calif. 94558.

Utlas, Inc., 80 Bloor Street W., 2nd Floor, Toronto, Ontario, Canada M5S 2V1.

Winnebago Software Co., 109 W. Main St., Caledonia, Minn. 55921.

WordPerfect Corp., 288 W. Center St., Orem, Utah 84057. 801-227-4000.

Writing Consultants, Techniplex, 300 Main St., East Rochester, N.Y. 14445. 800-828-6293 or 716-377-0130.

Appendix C
Hardware-Software Cross Reference

The following is not a hardware requirements list; it is merely a quick guide to machine-version availability. For more information about memory requirements or model (e.g., XT, AT, PCjr.), check the hardware requirement section of the specific review. Consult the Index of Software for page references.

Apple II Series (Apple III in emulation mode)
Access
Accession Plus
Almanacs
AlphaChart
AppleWorks
AppleWorks for School
   Librarians
AppleWriter II
Art Prints Inventory
ASCII Express
AV Equipment Inventory
Bank Street Writer II
Bartlett's Familiar Quotations
Bibliography Writer
Book Trak I: Hard Disk Circulation System
Bookends
Card and Label Manager
Catalog Card and Label Writer
Catalog Card Maker III
Catalogit III
Cdex

Circulation Plus
Copy II+
Create
Crossword Magic
DB Master 4 Plus
dBase II (CP/M)
Diversi-Copy
Electronic Bookshelf
Elementary Library Media
   Skills
Essential Data Duplicator
Ettacq
Extra K
Fiction Finder
GBBS
Homeword
The Index
Ledgerit
Librarian's Helper
Library Circulation System
   I/II/III
LibraryWorks
List Handler
Mag-it

MICROsearch
Newsroom and Clip Art
Orderit
People's Message System
Perfect Writer
Personal Bibliographic System
PFS Family
Pinpoint
Prince
Print Shop
Puzzles and Posters
Readability Calculations
Reserve Power
Ripley's Library Research
  Skills
Sensible Grammar
Sensible Speller
Skills Maker
Smartcom I/II
SuperCalc
Templates—VisiCalc
Using an Index to Periodicals
Apple Macintosh
  Copy II MAC
  DB Master Macintosh
  Jazz
  MacWrite 4.5
  PFS Family
  Print Shop
  Professional Bibliographic
    System
  Smartcom I/II
Atari
  Crossword Magic
  Puzzles and Posters

Columbia
  Bib-Base/Acq
Commodore
  Accession Plus
  Catalog Card and Label
    Writer
  Crossword Magic

Homeword
The Index
Ledgerit
Mag-it
Newsroom
Orderit
PFS Family
Print Shop
Puzzles and Posters
Compaq
  CopyWrite
  PFS Family
CP/M
  ASCII Express (Apple)
  Librarian's Helper (Apple)
  MultiPlan (most systems)
  SuperCalc
  WordStar 3.3

DEC Rainbow
  InMagic/Biblio

IBM PC (and compatibles)
  Accession Plus
  Art Prints Inventory
  Art Studio
  ASCII Express
  Authex
  AV Equipment Inventory
  Bank Street Writer II
  BBS-PC
  Bib-Base/Acq
  BiblioFile
  Card and Label Manager
  Catalog Card and Label
    Writer
  Catalogit III
  Cdex
  Circulation Manager
  Circulation Plus
  Copy II PC
  CopyWrite
  Create

Crossword Magic
DB Master
dBase II
dBase III
FILLS
Framework II
GBBS
Grammatik II
GRCComQuest
Homeword
The Index
InfoQUEST OPAC
InMagic/Biblio
Ledgerit
Librarian's Helper
Lotus 1-2-3
Mag-it
MATSS
Micro-CAIRS
MultiPlan
Newsroom and Clip Art
Orderit
OutputM
PC/Net LINK
Perfect Writer
PFS Family
Print Shop
Pro-Cite
Professional Bibliographic
  System
ProSearch
Puzzles and Posters
Readability Calculations
Serial Control System
SideKick
Smartcom I/II
SuperCalc
Word Finder

WordPerfect
WordStar 2000

M300
  BiblioFile
  GRCComQuest
  Pro-Cite
  Professional Bibliographic
    System

TRS-80 III or IV
  Scripsit/SuperScripsit
  SuperCalc

TRS-80 III or IV
  Art Prints Inventory
  AV Equipment Inventory
  Bibliography Writer
  Catalog Card and Label
    Writer
  Circulation Plus
  The Index
  Puzzles and Posters
TRS/Tandy 1000
  Bib-Base/Acq
TRS/Tandy 1200
  Circulation Plus
TRS/Tandy 2000
  Cdex

Wang PC
  InMagic/Biblio

Zenith Z110/Z120
  Bib-Base/Acq
Zenith Z150/Z160
  Bib-Base/Acq
  CopyWrite

Glossary

ASCII – American Standard Code for Information Interchange. It represents 128 defined or agreed-upon characters in the binary code.

Backup – an extra copy maintained in case the primary disk or tape is destroyed.

Baud – the speed at which information travels. 300 baud is 30 characters per second; 1200 baud is 120 characters per second.

Binary – pertaining to the code of the computer, which is based on two numbers: 0 and 1.

Bit – the smallest piece of computer information, literally a 1 or 0. By adding bits in units of eight, the computer forms bytes, each of which represents a character. 128 of these characters have been defined as ASCII code.

Boilerplate – in word processing, frequently used sections of text saved on disk and used to create new documents.

Buffer – a holding place or temporary storage area for text or other data. Special RAM cards now exist that enhance RAM space for micros or function as a storage area for material sent to a printer. The computer is thereby freed for other work while the printing continues.

Bulletin Board System (BBS) – a computer database maintained on a micro or a mainframe. Users access it through a modem.

Byte – a word (character) for the computer, usually made up of 7, 8, or 10 bits, depending on whether stop and start or parity bits are used. The code for understanding what a byte means is ASCII, which defines the first 128 such bytes.

CP/M – Control Program for Microcomputers, the most widely used operating system available for micros. A large body of public domain software is available for it.

Cursor – the flashing or blinking marker on the screen or monitor which indicates where the next character will be typed.

Cut and Paste – the electronic word processing function analogous to the editorial practice of physically cutting and reorganizing paper manuscript.

Database – an organized collection of data (facts, information, words) that can be accessed either locally or remotely by telephone with the aid of a modem.

Disk Drive – the mechanical device which reads and writes data on a disk or diskette.

153

Documentation—instructions for using the computer. It may be printed, online, or even a tape recording.

DOS—Disk Operating System.

Dot Matrix—print composed of a cluster (matrix) of dots. Some dot matrix printers now use overlapping dots in order to produce "near letter quality" print, close to that of daisywheel printers.

Download—to receive data from another computer remotely (through the telephone with the aid of a modem).

File—a collection of data stored on a disk. Files are organized in many different ways, depending upon the use and program. A word processing file may contain only text, or it may contain many "dot" commands that format the text when it is printed out. Some programs prepare files in a special way, making them incompatible with other programs.

Graphics—a two-dimensional representation. Computers can handle high-resolution graphics made up of small dots (like a TV picture) or low-resolution graphics made up of larger blocks. High resolution requires more memory space.

Hardcopy—printed copy.

Icon—a picture or drawing representing some action. A hand with a pen may represent word processing, etc.

Integrated Software—software that will work together in some way. Most integrated software will have word processing, database management, spreadsheet functions, and sometimes graphics and telecommunications, all combined. Users may swap files or switch functions without exiting the program. Some integrated software packages are known as software "families," which means that they are programs from the same vendor which, although compatible, may still require that the user exit one in order to "boot up" another.

Macro—in automatic typing, a predefined set of characters executed at the touch of a single key or code. Some macros are used to avoid retyping a long or complicated term or phrase; others are used in telecommunications to dial a telephone number or enter log-on codes or even an entire search pattern.

Mailmerge—to merge two files, typically a form letter and a name and address file, to produce a custom product. A word processor function.

Megabyte—one million bytes.

Menu—a selection or set of choices on the computer screen. A menu-driven program is usually easier to use than a command-driven program, since it supplies a list of options from which to choose. Command-driven programs offer no selection and the command set must be memorized.

Modem—literally MODulator/DEModulator. Modems change the binary code of the computer into the analog code of the telephone system and back again. In this way, computers can communicate over the telephone.

Monitor—the screen which displays the computer output.

Network—two or more micros connected by telephone or direct wiring; usually they share some functions.

Operating System—the set of programs that control the microcomputer. CP/M is one example of a popular operating system. A computer may use more than one operating system.

Optical Disk—external data storage that utilizes a laser. Its great advantage is that it is capable of storing enormous amounts of data on a single disk.

Parallel Transmission—information or data flow that sends data eight bits at one time (or parallel). Serial, on the other hand, sends data one bit at a time, single file.

Peripheral—a device or accessory not part of the computer proper: printers, modems, graphics tablets, etc.

Protocol—a method for sending error-free files between two computers at high speeds. Without a protocol, errors introduced by the imperfections of the telephone system might go unnoticed and uncorrected. Different kinds of protocols exist, and so the two computers sending and receiving files must use the same protocol. Christensen (Xmodem) protocol is the most widespread and popular.

RAM—Random Access Memory. Synonymous with temporary storage. Programs and data are loaded into this space and erased when finished.

Record—a single entry in a file. A record is comprised of fields. For instance, an address file would contain many records. Each record would consist of several fields: name, address, city, state, and zip code. A set of records is called a file.

ROM—Read Only Memory. A collection of fixed, non-alterable programs that the computer has permanently stored in its chips.

Save—to store data on disk.

Serial Transmission—data sent one bit at a time, single file. Data sent eight bits simultaneously is parallel.

Softcopy—data viewed on the screen instead of printed out on a printer (hardcopy).

Spreadsheet—the electronic equivalent of the accountant's paper and pen. The use of electronic spreadsheets makes "what if" statements quick and easy by allowing the input of many different combinations of data.

Telecommunications—the sending and receiving of data over the telephone with the aid of a modem.

Template—any predefined form that can be modified and reused for other purposes. Template resembles boilerplate, but it is generally reserved to describe spreadsheet files.

Upload—to send a file to another computer through the telephone line with the aid of a modem.

Word Wrap—in word processing, the end-of-line situation in which the text continues around to the next line, instead of halting or waiting for a carriage return.

Index of Applications

157

Index of Software

Patrick R. Dewey is administrative librarian of the Maywood (Ill.) Public Library. He previously held the position of branch head and reference librarian in the Chicago Public Library System. For the past two years Dewey has edited a software reviewing column in *Wilson Library Bulletin*: he is the author of *Public Access Microcomputers: A Handbook for Librarians* (KIPI, 1984). Dewey also has published articles in *American Libraries, Public Libraries, Library Journal, School Library Journal, Electronic Libraries, Library Software Review, Modem Notes, Library Hi-Tech, Popular Computing,* and *Small Computers in Libraries.*